First published 1979 by Octopus Books Limited
59, Grosvenor Street, London W.1.

© 1979 Octopus Books Limited

ISBN 7064 · 0966 · 3
D. L. To-688-79

Printed in Spain by Artes Gráficas Toledo, S. A.

Play Better Bridge

with Rixi Markus

Foreword by Omar Sharif

Play Better Bridge

I welcome another book about bridge by Rixi Markus whom I have known for many years as a player and as a writer. I always enjoy listening to what she has to say and as a writer she has a highly original style. She has her own ideas about bidding as the reader can judge. Although one can sometimes disagree with her, it cannot be denied that she has been the most successful woman player in the world and that her books have been enjoyed by all those who have read them.

This new book is a collection of hands which will interest readers and also enlighten them about many new and old ideas in that famous Rixi style. Easy to read, easy to understand and never boring.

Omar Sharif

When I was approached by the publishers of this book and asked to write 70,000–75,000 words and was told that the book would have to include many pictures and at least 200 bridge hands, my first reaction was that I could not possibly face such a task. An unfortunate ski accident, however, gave me plenty of time to consider the proposal and I then decided to accept. It seemed a kind of challenge.

I do hope that my readers will be able to understand most of what I am trying to convey to them in all these chapters. Namely that you can play bridge without wasting too much effort. Bridge should be a relaxation and a pleasure and not a torture. Therefore I am trying to explain certain principles which although not too easy to learn eventually help you to master the game which appears at first so difficult.

I advise you to adopt those principles which appeal to you and to ignore the rest. There is something for everyone in this book. It can help you to improve your own game and you can also be entertained by the experiences of the masters.

I was very lucky to find a most efficient collaborator in one of our young experts, Eric Crowhurst, who provided some of the material and also typed the manuscript with such perfection that very few corrections were needed.

R. Markus

Questions & Answers

QUESTIONS AND ANSWERS

I travel a great deal in my bridge life, and international bridge events these days are staged in a variety of attractive places. In the course of my travels I must meet thousands of players, and I have had a marvellous opportunity to watch the way in which the game has been developing in recent years. It is not so long ago that bridge was a game for the privileged classes, mainly played by those who could afford to spend their leisure time at their clubs or at private gatherings of lovers of the game. The scene has now completely changed. A recent survey showed that about 50 million people all over the world are currently playing bridge, and the pleasures of the game are now available to almost everybody.

Many of the players whom I meet at bridge events ask me about my views on various aspects of the game. Since a number of these questions seem to recur fairly regularly, it may be of interest if I run quickly through the most common of them, together with my answers.

QUESTION: How can I improve my game? I have been playing for quite a long time, but I seem to be making very little progress.

ANSWER: As in all sports, the best way to improve your game is to play with others who are at least as good as, and preferably better than, you. If this does not seem to do any good, try to watch the great players in action and to participate in tournaments where you are bound to meet a number of experts. The important point is that you must not be afraid of playing with or against the top players. Courage is one of the main qualities required to do well at this fascinating game, and you will never get very far if you are afraid.

QUESTION: What do you think makes a good bridge player?

ANSWER: In my view, playing bridge is very similar to playing a musical instrument: you can reach a very acceptable standard by sheer perseverance. Even if you lack a special talent for the game, you can make up for it by practising as much as you can and by listening to those who know better. Humility is a great asset in bridge; obstinacy is a great handicap.

QUESTION: What are the special qualities or talents required by a good bridge player?

ANSWER: A top-ranking champion needs a large number of different qualities, but just a few of the vital ingredients will be sufficient to elevate you into the near-expert class. The first basic requirement is an ability to count, preferably as high as 52. Let me give you an example from a recent Individual contest. I was faced by a lady who managed on one hand to bid no trumps before I had a chance to. Her diamond suit in 3NT was as follows:

DUMMY	DECLARER
◇A K 9 8 6 4	◇J 10 7 5

Her first move was to run ◇J and lose to the singleton ◇Q in the North hand. Not only could she not resist a finesse, she also could not count, and I simply had to point out to her that, since there are only thirteen cards in each suit and she could see ten diamonds in her two hands, she was certain to make all six diamond tricks once South had followed suit on the first round.

This is, of course, an extreme example, but I cannot emphasise too strongly the importance of counting in bridge. Whether you are attempting to keep track of high-card points, tricks, distributions or opponents' hands, accurate counting at all times is vital.

The second basic quality needed to become a good bridge player is an ability to concentrate. Just as if you are driving a car, your eyes and ears must be fully occupied with the task in hand at all times; you simply must ignore everything which might distract you. You should be trying all the time to build up a mental picture of the unseen hands, deriving all the clues you possibly can from the bidding and from the play of the cards. Don't for one second think of anything but those 52 cards.

Good psychology is another useful asset at the bridge table. If you understand the characters of your partner and your opponents, you will find it much easier to assess their actions than if you were playing with or against complete strangers.

Don't be obstinate during the bidding. If partner seems reluctant to allow you to play in your five- or six-card suit, trust him to know best. He will not always be right, but it will pay you in the long run not to argue with partner. Mutual confidence is of great importance in any successful partnership, and two moderate players can often do better than two experts who treat each other with less respect.

Self-confidence is necessary in bridge, but it must not be allowed to turn into conceit; as I said before, humility is a useful asset. I believe that one can always find the most obstinate players at their very worst in Individual contests, where they pay their table money and feel free to get rid of all their inhibitions.

House of Lords versus *House of Commons for the* Guardian *Trophy. Sir Harwood Harrison and Harold Lever watched by Rixi Markus against Lord Payer and Lord Grimthorpe.*

QUESTIONS AND ANSWERS

(Fig. I)

```
              ♠ A 9 8
              ♡ K 6 4 2
              ◇ J 2
              ♣ K Q J 3

♠ J                        ♠ Q 10 6 4 2
♡ A 10 9 8 7 3    N        ♡ J
◇ K 6 3       W       E    ◇ Q 9 5
♣ 10 9 5          S        ♣ A 7 6 4

              ♠ K 7 5 3
              ♡ Q 5
              ◇ A 10 8 7 4
              ♣ 8 2
```

Mention of Individual contests gives me an opportunity to put into print some of my views on this controversial subject. I personally find Individuals most annoying, and I only play in them under protest. The Individual in the Chamonix Bridge Festival in September 1978 was a case in point. I actually succeeded in winning the event, but I still did not really enjoy the game. A large number of my partners, particularly the ladies seemed to go to great lengths to play hands which really belonged to me, and I find that this is often the case in this kind of competition.

However, there was one hand from Chamonix which I enjoyed. North dealt at love all (see Fig. I).

The bidding at my table was as follows:

NORTH	EAST	SOUTH	WEST
1♣	NB	1♠ (1)	2♡
2♠	NB	NB	NB

(1) I have always found that French players like you to show a four-card major suit at every conceivable opportunity.

West led ♡A and another heart. East ruffed and, faced with an awkward return, switched to ◇5. I ducked to West's ◇K, and West returned ♡10 which I covered with dummy's ♡K. East ruffed with ♠10, and I overruffed with ♠K and led a club to the king and ace. East returned a club, and I felt that the time had come to play a round of trumps. When ♠A dropped the jack from West, the picture became clear. I cashed another trump in dummy and ruffed dummy's last club with my small spade. I then cashed ◇A, ruffed a diamond and led a heart from dummy. By this time, East only had trumps left, but he could not prevent me from making ♠7 as my eighth trick. +110 gave me the second best score on the board.

Individual contests are renowned for the strange and unexpected results which occur on almost every board. The reason clearly is that you are playing most of the time with and against complete strangers, some of them mere beginners, some of them of average standard and some of them very reasonable players with a masochistic streak. The difficulty lies in assessing the capabilities of your partner in time, for you may have to take emergency action to prevent him from playing a contract which is likely to prove too difficult for him.

Here is a typical incident from Chamonix 1978. West dealt at love all (see Fig. II).

(II)

```
              ♠ K J 9
              ♡ Q 9 8 7 3
              ◇ 8 3
              ♣ A 8 7

♠ Q 10 6 3                 ♠ A 8 7
♡ A 10 6      N            ♡ K J 4
◇ A Q 6       W       E    ◇ J 10 2
♣ Q 9 2           S        ♣ K J 6 5

              ♠ 5 4 2
              ♡ 5 2
              ◇ K 9 7 5 4
              ♣ 10 4 3
```

WEST	NORTH	EAST	SOUTH
1♣ (1)	1♡	2◇ (2)	Double (3)
NB	NB	NB	

(1) East-West were playing five-card majors, about which I shall have more to say in a later chapter.
(2) A strange choice; 3NT would seem more natural.
(3) I don't like to be shut completely out of these auctions.

Believe it or not, we managed to hold declarer to eight tricks, restricting our loss to −180. When we opened the travelling score sheet, we found that we would still have scored a complete "top" even if East had managed to make two overtricks, for every other East-West pair had made ten or eleven tricks in 3NT, scoring +430 or +460.

It is difficult to understand why East chose to bid 2◇ in the first place; it is even more difficult to understand why he elected to stick it out when 2◇ was doubled. Perhaps you will now believe me when I say that anything is possible in an Individual contest. Individuals teach one a lot about the psychology of the game and its players.

I am afraid I have rather strayed from the point, but whenever the word "Individual" is mentioned, I can never resist telling one or two stories about some of the amazing things that have happened to me over the years. Now back to the main theme of this chapter.

QUESTION: You have always played with a number of different partners. How do you manage to get on so well with so many partners?
ANSWER: If you want to achieve the best possible results, either in competition bridge or rubber bridge, I have always believed that your attitude towards your partner is almost as important as your technical skill at the game. If you are playing with a partner less skilful than yourself, try to give him confidence by trusting him and ignoring his errors, especially when he is confronted by problems with which he could not hope to cope. Even if you feel that you would have done much better than he did, refrain from saying so; to point this out at the table will almost certainly make him play even worse on future hands, and it will be much better in the long run if you show patience and understanding.

Playing the 'silent partner'

The best approach is to keep quiet and show no reaction at the table. If you feel that you simply must say something, restrict yourself to some such comment as: "Never mind. It was a very difficult situation." If you wish to discuss certain hands with your partner, wait until the end of the session. Even then it must be a *partnership* discussion, and you must never overlook the possibility that some of the mistakes might be partially or entirely your fault.

Earlier in this chapter, I compared playing bridge with playing a musical instrument, and this analogy also applies to the way in which you handle your partner. A true artist will get the best tune out of any instrument, and a vital part of being a good bridge player is the ability to persuade your partner to play his best.

Those of you who know me well will not be surprised when I say that I myself have a difficult temperament. However, I have learnt from bitter experience that it pays me to control my temper at the table: the more I control it, the better my results are. In my particular case, it needs a great effort to maintain my self-control, but you must believe me—it's worth it.

I have played with a large number of partners during my bridge career. Many of them were excellent players, but others have been those who play the game for enjoyment—particularly at rubber bridge. These casual players may not have mastered the finer points of the game, but you must not spoil their pleasure by criticising their lack of skill; they generally do their best, and they will almost always do even better with a little encouragement from you.

Two more important points on handling indifferent partners. Don't be selfish and don't try to play every hand: if you do, you will often find yourself in the wrong contract or, more often, in the right contract played from the wrong side of the table. Secondly, don't create problems for your partner in the bidding or in the defence; you will be suitably rewarded if you keep everything as simple as possible.

I personally believe that I show much more tolerance towards the weaker players than I do towards the so-called "experts", especially when the latter attack me unjustly. I am always quite prepared to admit to my mistakes, but I sometimes react violently when I am wrongly accused. I have been trying for a long time to improve my own conduct at the table, and I always start each session full of good intentions. However, there are certain players who know how to irritate me, and my results generally suffer accordingly. In fact, I know several players who can play perfect bridge until something irritating happens, but who then almost invariably commit a series of elementary blunders.

Nobody is perfect

I always explain to any partner who is disappointed with our performance that you can never hope to achieve 100% in a game which contains so many mysteries and problems. In pairs tournaments, of course, a score of 65% is excellent and, while it is possible on a lucky day and in an uneven field to reach 75%, this is only feasible if you have much more than your fair share of good fortune. In team events, it is fairly common to record larger percentage scores, for a strong team can crush a weaker one and pile on the points at both tables.

To summarise my views on how to handle partners, I would say that there must always be a sympathetic relationship in a partnership which is working well. This simply means that you must feel genuinely sorry when your partner fails to find the best bid or the best solution to a cardplay problem. If you are tolerant and understanding, your partner's performance will improve noticeably; if you show contempt or disapproval, any mistakes which he makes on subsequent hands will be to a large extent *your* fault.

Bridge Today

There was a time when I used to resent being called "Rixi Markus—the bridge player". Nowadays, however, I realise just how much the game has given me, and I feel now that I can wear that particular label with pride. I also believe that I am qualified to give a little advice to any of you who enjoy the game of bridge as much as I do.

Looking back, I realise how close I was to becoming a complete bridge fanatic, treating the game as nothing less than an obsession. You must be careful that this never happens to you; otherwise you will subsequently regret you neglected life's other enjoyments.

My green baize war

The only period of my life in which I allowed bridge to take over was during the Second World War. There was at that time very little that a person in my position could do and, although I did Civil Defence duties and helped with secretarial and book-keeping work in various offices, I still had plenty of time, day and night, to sit at that green baize table for four. We found that the fireworks at the bridge table helped to take our minds off the bombs and explosions outside, and the game helped to bring everybody closer together. In fact, bridge in those days was much more pleasant and less hostile than it is today. I managed to win a lot of money at that time, but I never felt that anyone was jealous or begrudged me my success. The result was that I enjoyed winning much more then than I do nowadays, when so many players seem to be too eager and too greedy.

After the war, I soon realised that I was playing too much bridge, and I immediately cut down on my sessions or made them of shorter duration. I had many other activities to pursue, and I was determined not to allow bridge to take over completely.

In those days, I enjoyed rubber bridge just as much as the tournament game, and I still regard rubber bridge in top-class company as my favourite pastime. There are still millions of people playing rubber bridge today, but tournament bridge has made enormous strides in recent years. In fact, I find personally that, with my life divided between writing about bridge and playing in exciting international festivals in attractive venues all over the world, I have very little time left in which to enjoy a game of rubber bridge. To my great regret, my bridge "at the club" has virtually come to an end these days, largely because of my work on books and articles.

A great British future

(III) Dealer South; North-South vulnerable.

```
                ♠ Q 9 7 3
                ♡ A 5 4
                ◇ J 10 7
                ♣ 8 6 3
  ♠ 8 6                         ♠ K 10 5 4 2
  ♡ Q J 10 6      N             ♡ 9 8 2
  ◇ Q 8 6 4    W     E          ◇ 9 3 2
  ♣ K J 4         S             ♣ 9 7
                ♠ A J
                ♡ K 7 3
                ◇ A K 5
                ♣ A Q 10 5 2
```

As you will probably have gathered already, I shall be doing quite a lot of looking back in this book, and I shall actually be devoting a later chapter to remembering some of the great players of the past. However, I would also like to take a quick look ahead to the future of bridge in this country, and I am pleased to say that we have recently had a significant success to celebrate in this connection. In August 1978, the Great Britain team won the Junior European Championship for the first time ever. This event, which was held at Stirling University in Scotland, was contested by nineteen countries, and the British team was Michael Rosenberg and Richard Benstead, Richard Granville and Tony Forrester, and Michael Nardin and Stephen Lodge; Keith Stanley was the non-playing captain.

Michael Rosenberg has actually left this country and gone to live in the USA, but he came back to help his team win the Championship and he undoubtedly proved to be the star performer. Here is a hand from the match against Belgium which would have given many expert players a severe headache; Rosenberg solved the problem easily (see Fig. III).

Rosenberg opened 2NT with the South hand, his partner raised to 3NT and everybody passed. West led ♡Q and South won the second round with the king. Unwilling to waste the vital entry to dummy in order to bank everything on a successful club guess, he began by leading ♣A and ♣Q. West won and continued with a heart to dummy's ace, and declarer now had to decide whether to take the spade finesse or the diamond finesse for his ninth trick. Fortunately for Great Britain, he played a spade to ♠J and knocked out West's ♣J. West was able to cash one heart trick, but South now had nine tricks. You may think that Rosenberg was lucky to take the spade finesse rather than the diamond finesse, but I always believe that a true champion makes his own luck. There is, in fact, a definite advantage in playing on spades. If ♠J loses and West is unable to cash the thirteenth heart, declarer still has a chance of dropping ♢Q in two rounds; on the other hand, if South were to take an unsuccessful diamond finesse first, he would only have the slim chance of the singleton ♠K to fall back on.

At the other table, the Belgium declarer in 3NT won the heart lead with dummy's ace and played a club to the ten. West won and persevered with hearts. South now cleared the clubs but found himself squeezed when West cashed the thirteenth heart. If he threw a spade or a diamond, West would exit in that suit; and if he threw a winning club, a spade switch by West would leave declarer with only eight tricks.

Sterling Stirling success

Great Britain's victory in Stirling was the first European success by a male British team for fifteen years, and this must augur well for the future. We women have done considerably better during that period, and I feel glad and proud that I have been able to contribute to a number of triumphs in the European Ladies' Championship, in partnership with Doris, Lady Rhodes, Marjory Whittaker, Fritzi Gordon and others.

One of my proudest moments in bridge was in Palermo in 1959, when the British Women's Team won the European Championship and I received an extra medal as the best lady player in the tournament. Most top bridge players are vain, although by no means all of them would admit to vanity. I am quite prepared to confess that I am vain, but I do not think that I am conceited. However, I felt a little upset when I got back from Palermo and found that my special award had not been mentioned in our bridge publications. You can therefore imagine my surprise and delight when the British champion, Claude Rodrigue, wrote an extremely flattering account of my achievement in the January 1960 issue of the *Bridge World* magazine. I quote:

"A surprisingly little publicised result from the European Championships at Palermo was that a member of our Ladies' Team won the award for the best woman player. By popular ballot, this title went to Mrs. Rixi Markus. Intrigued by this lack of interest in the bridge press, I obtained a copy of the records and what I saw confirmed that Rixi (overlooked of recent years) had swept through Palermo on the crest of a wave."

Rodrigue continued in a most flattering manner, and quoted a number of hands which he had found in the records. One of them is my favourite hand from Palermo, and it occurred at a critical stage of our crucial match against Belgium (see Fig. IV, overleaf).

(IV)

```
              ♠ K 8
              ♡ 8 2
              ◇ K Q J 10 9
              ♣ A K 3 2
♠ 7 4 2                        ♠ A J 10
♡ 10 7 6 3      N             ♡ K Q J 5
◇ 6 5 3 2    W   E            ◇ 8 4
♣ 10 4          S             ♣ Q 9 7 5
              ♠ Q 9 6 5 3
              ♡ A 9 4
              ◇ A 7
              ♣ J 8 6
```

The bidding at my table was as follows:

NORTH	EAST	SOUTH	WEST
Mrs. Whittaker		Mrs. Markus	
1◇	Double	Redouble	1♡
NB	2♡	2♠	NB
3♣	NB	3◇	NB
3♠	NB	4♠	NB
NB	Double	NB	NB
NB			

West led ♣10 against 4♠ doubled. I won in dummy with ♣A and made the key play of ♠8 from dummy. East was forced to duck, and I was able to win with ♠Q and turn my attention to diamonds. Nothing could save East now, for I was able to take my discards on the diamonds whether she ruffed or not, and this restricted the defenders to two spade tricks and one heart.

Returning now to our recent success in the Junior European Championships, it is important to remember that Great Britain was only able to stage those championships because of the great efforts of Mr. and Mrs. Charles Bowman and because of the generous financial support provided by David Mack, M.B.E., the General Manager of the National Bank of Dubai. It has become so expensive to run such events these days that we all depend to a large extent on the support of the generous sponsors who have moved into the world of bridge in recent years. I have personally been involved in several sponsored contests: the *Guardian* Easter Tournament, which has now grown into a ninety-table event with competitors from more than twenty countries, the December *Harper's-Queen's* Tournament, the *Evening Standard* Charity Congress, the Helena Rubinstein Women's Teams Championship, and finally the annual *Guardian* Trophy match between the House of Lords and the House of Commons. This last event is always a fascinating rubber bridge duplicate match, and the Commons are currently 3–1 up in the series. This is due to a considerable extent to the efforts of their star player, the Rt. Hon. Harold Lever, whose sparkling cardplay and inveterate overbidding will be remembered by members of the old Hamilton Club. Here he is in action in the 1978 Lords v. Commons match (see Fig. V).

In one room, the Commons' North-South pair played peacefully in 3NT, making nine tricks and winning a 700-point rubber. At the other table, however, Harold Lever was very much in the action.

(V) Dealer West; North-South vulnerable

```
              ♠ 8 7 5
              ♡ 9 8 5
              ◇ 4 2
              ♣ A K Q J 10
♠ Q 6 4 2                     ♠ K J 9
♡ K 10 4 2      N             ♡ Q 7 6
◇ Q 10 9 3   W   E            ◇ J 8 7 6 5
♣ 8             S             ♣ 6 4
              ♠ A 10 3
              ♡ A J 3
              ◇ A K
              ♣ 9 7 5 3 2
```

WEST	NORTH	EAST	SOUTH
Lever			
NB	NB	NB	1♣
Double	Redouble	1◇	1NT
2◇	3NT	NB	NB
4◇	Double	NB	NB
NB			

To make three bids on a seven-point hand when your partner has not made a single positive move is not bad going, but this excellent sacrifice cost only 300 points and saved the rubber.

Although the House of Commons currently has a comfortable lead in the series, the Lords' team has recently been considerably strengthened by the arrival of Lord Smith of Marlow—formerly Sir

Rodney Smith, the famous surgeon. Sir Rodney has long been a rubber bridge colleague of mine and, like Harold Lever, has a well-deserved reputation as a first-rate player of the cards. Here, for example, are two typical efforts by him:

```
              ♠J 10 7 6 5
              ♡Q J 8 4
              ◇A Q
              ♣A 5

  ♠A 3 2          N          ♠K
  ♡10 7 5 3    W     E       ♡9 6 2
  ◇9 8            S          ◇7 6 5 3 2
  ♣9 8 4 2                   ♣Q J 10 6

              ♠Q 9 8 4
              ♡A K
              ◇K J 10 4
              ♣K 7 3
```

On this occasion, Sir Rodney was playing with the late Karel Stepanek, the actor and keen rubber bridge player . . . and optimist.

SOUTH	WEST	NORTH	EAST
1NT	NB	2♣	NB
2♠	NB	4◇	NB
4♡	NB	6♠	NB
NB	NB		

This spirited auction left Sir Rodney with the difficult task of making a slam without the ace and king of trumps, but he found a neat deceptive play. West led ♣9, won in dummy with the ace. East played ♣10 as an encouraging card, but it would have clarified matters for his unfortunate partner if he had contributed ♣Q, thereby denying the king. South immediately played ◇A–Q, overtaking with ◇K, and led ◇J with the air of a man who was attempting to discard dummy's losing club. West ruffed low, and declarer overruffed in dummy, crossed back to hand with a heart and repeated the process by leading ◇10. West once again obliged by ruffing low, and declarer overruffed and led a round of trumps, crashing the ace and king together. East-West were still discussing this hand two days later.

(VI)

```
              ♠ J 10
              ♡ K Q 4
              ◇ A 10 6
              ♣ K J 9 5 3

♠ 7 2                        ♠ A 4
♡ J 10 7        N            ♡ A 9 8 6
◇ J 7 5 4 2   W   E          ◇ Q 8
♣ 10 4 2        S            ♣ A Q 8 7 6

              ♠ K Q 9 8 6 5 3
              ♡ 5 3 2
              ◇ K 9 3
              ♣ -
```

In my second example, (Fig. VI), Sir Rodney played well to take advantage of a greedy double.

EAST	SOUTH	WEST	NORTH
1♣	3♠	NB	3NT
Double	4♠	NB	NB
Double	NB	NB	NB

West led ♡J, and East captured the king with the ace and returned a second heart to dummy's queen. By this time, declarer had made his plan. He calculated that he needed to find one club honour and a long diamond suit in the West hand, and his first play was to lead ♣J from dummy and ruff away East's ♣Q. He then led a spade towards dummy, and East won with the ace, cashed a winning heart and exited with his second trump.

Declarer won in dummy and led ♣K, covered by East's ♣A and ruffed in hand. He then played out his remaining trumps, and the last spade squeezed the unfortunate West in the minor suits. His last four cards were three diamonds and ♣10 and, with dummy discarding after him, he could not help presenting declarer with his tenth trick.

Sponsorships as I outlined above have become a prominent feature of present-day bridge. Another even more recent development, and in my view a far less desirable one, is what I call "play for pay"—that is, experts playing in partnership with so-called clients, who pay them their expenses and a fee for their services. This idea, like so many with a financial basis, was born in the USA, where certain lesser players were prepared to buy expert partners in their quest for Master Points. The trend has now spread to this country and to other parts of Europe, although the aim of the "clients" in our case seems to be the pursuit of prizes rather than Master Points.

The professional menace

I must say that I do not like to see professionalism of this kind creeping into our bridge life. To some extent, however, the new practice is understandable. In some countries, such as Great Britain, the USA and Sweden, tournament organisers are not permitted to give money rewards. In most other European countries, however, including those in the Communist Bloc, there are substantial cash prizes, and to play with an expert partner is probably the only chance some of the poorer players will ever have of taking a share of the proceeds. Furthermore, the tournaments which offer huge prizes also charge very high entry fees, and some of the better players from this country can ill-afford to play abroad at their own expense; they are therefore delighted to find clients who are prepared to pay their travelling expenses and entry money, plus a fee for playing with them. One of the unfortunate consequences of this professionalism is, of course, that many of our best tournament players are rarely available to practise with their regular partners, and this must inevitably weaken the playing strength of our national teams.

I personally am very lucky in that I have never needed to play in a professional capacity. As a bridge journalist and reasonably well-known writer, I frequently receive invitations to play in attractive international bridge festivals—and I am always free to select either a good friend or a good player, or both, as my partner. And they do not have to pay me.

The Stage is Yours

Tips on Bidding in an Uncontested Auction

THE STAGE IS YOURS

There is so much that one can say about constructive bidding and, just as in politics, every expert has his own views and ideas. This must make it difficult for the average player to decide which are the best methods for him and whom he should follow.

I am a very independent person, and I have formulated one or two strict theories of bidding of my own which I always follow. Sometimes, of course, I come severely unstuck and wish that I had been a little less dogmatic, but I believe that it pays in the long run to establish one's own set of bidding principles and then stick to them as far as possible.

Here are some of my basic principles of bidding in uncontested sequences; in Chapter 4, I shall go on to set out my tips on bidding when the opponents are also taking an active part in the auction.

(1) *Don't play too many gadgets: keep your brain fresh for the difficult problems which arise in play and defence.*

I have always preferred to play a relatively simple method of bidding, largely because I want to keep my brain fresh to deal with the tricky problems which always occur in playing and defending. My fear is that if my mind is burdened with a large number of gadgets, I shall continually be wondering how I could have introduced one of them into the auction, instead of concentrating fully on the job on hand: on preparing the way for a squeeze or endplay or on avoiding an unnecessary finesse.

Bidding a la carte

Having said that, I am by nature a tolerant person, and I think I can understand why so many of today's top players seem to want to play as many bidding conventions as possible. Whenever I come across these players, whose convention card looks like a menu in a very expensive restaurant, I follow their involved and intricate ways of reaching the obvious final contract with great curiosity, and I ask myself: Was their journey really necessary? Couldn't they have reached their final destination by a more direct route? However, bidding is clearly the department of the game which these players enjoy the most, and I would not wish to spoil their fun, provided that their bidding methods can be fairly easily interpreted for the benefit of any inexperienced opponents.

I do like to play one or two gadgets, principally (a) for slam-bidding purposes, when I employ cue bids and Blackwood, and (b) in response to an opening bid of 1NT, when I favour simple Stayman and Transfer Bids. Let me take this opportunity to say a few words about each of my favourite gadgets.

(i) *Cue bids and Blackwood.* It would be difficult to consider these two gadgets separately, for the bidding of the vast majority of slam contracts depends on the use of one or both of these devices. Among average players, Blackwood is used a lot; in fact, it is generally used much too much, and my view is that your slam bidding is bound to improve if you try to cue bid more often and only use Blackwood as a final check. Blackwood, in fact, should only be employed to keep you out of bad slams: good slams are much more likely to be reached by way of cue bids.

If you are contemplating the use of a Blackwood 4NT enquiry, stop and ask yourself one important question: "Shall I know what to do over any response from partner?" If the answer to this question is no, it is almost certain that you will do much better to initiate a cue-bidding sequence.

For example:

```
     SOUTH
♠ K Q 10 7 2        NORTH       EAST        SOUTH       WEST
♡ K 9 3             1♡          NB          1♠          NB
◇ 8 4               3♠          NB          ?
♣ A 10 2
```

Your excellent spade suit and good fit for partner's heart suit make this hand well worth a slam-going move after North's jump raise. However, this is definitely *not* a hand for Blackwood. If you bid 4NT and receive a reply of 5♡, showing two aces, you will still not know what to do.

If you jump to 6♠, you will find partner with two losing diamonds:

```
          NORTH
          ♠ A J 8 3
          ♡ A Q J 5 4
          ◇ Q 7
          ♣ K 4
```

and if you elect to sign off in 5♠ over 5♡, partner will probably pass and put down this kind of dummy:

```
          NORTH
          ♠ A 8 4 3
          ♡ A Q J 5 4
          ◇ K Q
          ♣ 7 4
```

As with so many hands of this nature, the answer is to cue bid. A bid of 4♣, showing ♣A, will alert partner to the fact that you are interested in slam possibilities. If he replies with 4◇, showing a diamond control, you can continue with 4♡, showing your key card in his suit. If he bids 4♡ over 4♣, showing ♡A and denying ◇A, you are probably worth a jump to 5♠, which will indicate two losing cards in the unbid suit; North can then push on to 6♠ if he has second-round control in diamonds.

(II) *Stayman*. Stayman is another convention in very common use. It entails the use of an artificial 2♣ response to 1NT, asking the opener to show a four-card major suit if he has one. It seems to me that some kind of gadget along these lines is absolutely vital, for it is otherwise difficult to see how you can hope to reach the correct contract on hands of this type:

```
     WEST                EAST
♠ K J 7 2           ♠ A 9 6 5
♡ A 4               ♡ 7 6
◇ K 10 8 3          ◇ Q J 7 2
♣ A Q 6             ♣ K 8 3
```

West opens with a strong 1NT, showing 16–18 points. East clearly has the values for game, but he has no way of showing his suits: 2◇ or 2♠ would be weak, non-forcing responses, and 3◇ or 3♠ would guarantee at least a five-card suit. In the absence of any conventional methods, therefore, East would have to raise to 3NT, which will be defeated by an opening heart lead. Stayman solves the problem. East makes a 2♣ enquiry, West shows his four-card spade suit, and East raises to 4♠—the correct game contract.

(iii) *Transfer Bids.* Transfer Bids in response to an opening bid of 1NT constitute one of the most important developments in bidding technique to be made in recent years. In its simplest form, this method involves a response of 2♢, which asks the opener to convert to 2♡, and a response of 2♡, requesting a conversion to 2♠. The obvious advantage of this is that it permits the stronger hand to become the declarer if the responder has a weak hand with a long major suit.

SOUTH
♠ Q J 7 5 3
♡ 6 4
♢ Q 9 8 3
♣ 7 2

If North opens 1NT (16–18 points), South can bid 2♡ to arrange for North to play in the safe contract of 2♠. This will mean that the opening lead is coming up to, rather than through, the strong hand and its tenaces; it also means that the stronger hand will be concealed, and this will almost certainly make things more difficult for the defence.

Let us strengthen the above hand slightly.

SOUTH
♠ Q J 7 5 3 2
♡ 6 4
♢ K 10 9 4
♣ 2

South is now worth a game bid opposite a strong 1NT, and his obvious move under normal methods would be to jump to 4♠. Playing Transfer Bids, however, he can bid 2♡ and raise to 4♠ over North's compulsory conversion to 2♠; this will once again ensure that the opening lead does not come through the strong hand.

Another advantage of Transfer Bids is that it makes it easier to describe essentially balanced hands containing a five-card major suit. For example:

SOUTH
♠ 7 2
♡ K 10 7 5 3
♢ A 9 5
♣ 10 8 7

If North opens 1NT, showing 16–18 points, this type of holding is difficult to handle under traditional methods. A bid of 2♡ would be a mere rectification of the final contract and would not show any positive values; but a jump to 3♡ would be forcing to game and would be a distinct exaggeration on this moderate hand. The two possible solutions are to make a quantitative raise to 2NT, ignoring the five-card heart suit, or to bid 2♣, Stayman, and follow with a game-try bid of 3♡, risking toppling overboard if partner has a doubleton heart and 2NT is the only makeable contract.

Rixi Markus during a bridge event.

Transfer Bids solve this problem neatly. South bids 2◇, North obliges with 2♡, and South converts to 2NT. This shows a balanced raise to 2NT containing a five-card heart suit, and North should now be in a good position to choose the best final contract, whether it be 2NT, 3NT, 3♡ or 4♡.

One final example of the improved bidding technique which follows from the use of Transfer Bids over 1NT.

```
           SOUTH
         ♠ Q 10 6 5 4
         ♡ 6
         ◇ A K 7 2
         ♣ 9 8 7
```

This hand is clearly worth game opposite a 16–18 1NT, but South has no means of describing it accurately under normal methods. He has to start with a jump to 3♠ to show a five-card suit and create a game-forcing situation, but there is now no room in which to mention the diamonds without venturing beyond 3NT. Once again Transfer Bids make things much easier. South bids 2♡, North converts to 2♠, and South rebids 3◇. This sequence shows five spades, at least four diamonds, and good values, and North should again be well placed to select the best final contract.

THE STAGE IS YOURS

(Fig. I)

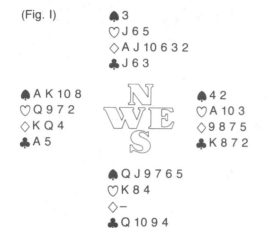

♠ 3
♡ J 6 5
◇ A J 10 6 3 2
♣ J 6 3

♠ A K 10 8
♡ Q 9 7 2
◇ K Q 4
♣ A 5

♠ 4 2
♡ A 10 3
◇ 9 8 7 5
♣ K 8 7 2

♠ Q J 9 7 6 5
♡ K 8 4
◇ –
♣ Q 10 9 4

So much for the gadgets which I like. My pet hates are the Weak Two, the Weak One No Trump when vulnerable, the Mini No Trump, and, most of all, the Multi-coloured Two Diamonds. This last convention is enjoying an unjustified spell of popularity these days, but my view is that its occasional successes occur only because the opponents have not bothered to devise effective counter-measures. The deal in Fig. I, from the 1978 Inter-Varsity match between Oxford and Cambridge is a good illustration of what I have in mind.

When the Cambridge University pair held the North-South cards, the bidding became a little confused, to say the least:

SOUTH	WEST	NORTH	EAST
2◇ (1)	NB (2)	2♡ (3)	NB
2♠ (4)	3♣ (5)	NB (6)	4♣ (7)
NB	4NT (8)	NB	5◇ (9)
NB	5♠ (10)	NB	6♣ (11)
NB	NB	NB	

(1) A Multi 2◇ opening, showing either (a) a weak 2♡, (b) a weak 2♠, (c) a very strong, balanced hand, or (d) a strong two bid in either minor suit; certain variations of the convention incorporate the ability to show a powerful 4–4–4–1 hand.

(2) I like to treat Weak Twos as one bids. For this reason, I would assume that the 2◇ is based on a Weak Two and make a natural overcall of 2NT on the West hand. Another defensive method against the Multi 2◇ is to double to suggest a penalty double of the opponents' eventual contract, and the West hand would be well suited to this treatment. As we shall see, West's actual decision to pass on the first round worked out extremely poorly.

(3) In principle, a negative reply. Assuming that his partner has a Weak Two bid, North has no wish to proceed beyond the two level.

(4) Showing a weak 2♠ opening.

(5) West now felt that the time had come for action, but it is still not clear why he did not make a penalty double of 2♠ or bid a natural 2NT. His actual choice of 3♣ was clearly meant to be a take-out bid, showing the other major.

(6) Relieved to be off the hook.

(7) East was confused. He clearly thought that his partner's 3♣ overcall was natural.

(8) West's 4NT bid was obviously meant to be natural, and not Blackwood . . .

(9) . . . but East showed one ace.

(10) West was still trying to escape and play the hand in 5NT . . .

(11) . . . but East thought that his partner was making a grand slam try. Understandably, he declined the invitation and signed off in six.

Oxford's gallant contract of 6♣ went three down, mercifully undoubled. West trapped himself by his original pass over 2◇, and this hand shows the kind of success which the Multi 2◇ opening can achieve if the opponents have not discussed beforehand how they are going to defend against it. Provided that you are armed in advance with effective counter-measures, the Multi 2◇ should really pose very few problems.

(2) *Always prepare your rebid before you open the bidding.*

I have always believed that the most common explanation for bidding disasters and poor auctions is that the opener omitted to prepare his rebid before he set the proceedings in motion. When you are contemplating an opening bid of one of a suit, you must always run through the possible responses your partner might produce and make sure that you can cope with them all without distorting your hand unnecessarily.

For example:

NORTH
♠ Q 7 2
♡ A K J 10
♢ 3 2
♣ K 7 5 4

1♡ is obviously the most descriptive opening bid on this hand. However, it is certainly not recommended, for what will you bid if partner makes the awkward response of 2♢? Playing the CAB system of rebids which I favour, you can rebid 2NT without showing additional values. Under normal Acol methods, however, a 2NT rebid in this situation would guarantee 15–16 points, and the correct opening bid in Acol is 1♣, not 1♡. Notice how 1♣ solves all rebid problems. Over 1♢, North can bid 1♡; over 1♡ or 1♠, he can raise to two of the major.

Similarly:

NORTH
♠ A J 10 4
♡ K 7 2
♢ A J 10 4
♣ 6 5

Moderate hands containing four spades and four diamonds are among the most difficult of all on which to select the correct opening bid, but the principle of looking ahead and catering for any response will always produce the winning answer. If North opens 1♢ on the above hand, for example, he will be poorly placed over a response of 2♣: 2♠ over 2♣ would be a reverse, showing a strong hand with at least five diamonds; 2NT would show 15–16 points, and 2♢ would guarantee at least five. The solution is to open the hand with 1♠. North can now rebid 2♢ over 2♣, raise 2♢ to 3♢, and raise to 3♡ over a response of 2♡, which is normally agreed to guarantee at least five hearts.

The fact that you might be faced with an insoluble rebid problem will sometimes dissuade you from opening at all.

NORTH
♠ A K Q
♡ 10 5 4 3 2
♢ 7 6 5
♣ K 4

Twelve points and a five-card major suit normally constitute an automatic opening bid, but I would certainly think twice before opening an Acol 1♡ bid on the above hand. A response of 2♣ or 2♢ will leave you in an extremely awkward position, for a rebid of 2NT would show at least three more points and a rebid of 2♡ on a suit of this quality would be extremely dangerous. There is therefore a great deal to be said for an original pass on this motley collection.

(3) *Don't open light unless you have a good suit.*
    This tip is really a corollary of the previous one. The fact that you have a good suit means that you will always have a descriptive rebid come what may, and you can therefore feel free to open a little light whenever the opportunity arises. For example, I would always open the bidding on the following hands:

♠ 6 5	♠ 7 4	♠ 7 5 4
♡ A Q J 9 5 4	♡ A K J 10 7	♡ K Q J 7 6 4
♢ 7	♢ K 8 4	♢ A 7 3
♣ K 10 7 5	♣ 7 5 2	♣ 2

1♡ cannot possibly come to any great harm on these hands, for you will be able to make the descriptive rebid of 2♡ over any response from partner.
    The quality of your suit should be the determining factor if you are contemplating a featherweight opening bid after two passes. To open light in third position can often work effectively and make things just a little more difficult for the opponents, but I feel strongly that you should only do so if you have a worthwhile suit.

♠ A 7 2	♠ A 7 2
♡ J 7 5 4 2	♡ K Q 10 9 4
♢ 6 4	♢ 6 4
♣ K Q 5	♣ 7 6 5
HAND A	HAND B

Hand A actually contains more high-card points than Hand B, but I would not dream of opening 1♡ on such a bad suit, even third in hand. After two passes, there is much more point in opening on Hand B: to open 1♡ may make it awkward for the opponents to get together, may make it difficult for them to play in no trumps, and will attract the best opening lead from your partner if your left-hand opponent eventually becomes the declarer. This last point is a particularly important one, for one of the main reasons for opening light should be to give partner a good opening lead; conversely, of course, it is extremely dangerous to bid a weak suit when it is almost certain that the opponents will eventually play the hand.

(4) *Don't count your points on distributionally powerful hands.*

I have always found that the Milton Work Point Count system works extremely well on balanced hands. On distributional hands, however, it is a great mistake to stick rigidly to counting your points—that is, unless you have discovered a reliable method of adding on extra points for voids, singletons and doubletons once you have found a fit.

As a good illustration of this fundamental point, consider this hand which appeared in *The Precision Club Newsletter*, no doubt as an advertisement for the accuracy of the system.

WEST	EAST
♠ J 7 4 2	♠ K Q 10 6 3
♡ 6	♡ Q 9 5
◇ A 8	◇ 7 6 4
♣ A K 10 6 5 4	♣ J 3

When this hand occurred in an important Vanderbilt Cup match in the USA, a pair playing the Precision Club system bid as follows to the correct contract:

WEST	EAST
2♣ (1)	2♠ (?)
4♠	NB

(1) Showing 11–15 points with either six clubs or at least five clubs with a four-card major suit.
(2) Non-forcing but constructive, showing at least five spades.

At the other table, a pair playing Standard American performed as follows:

WEST	EAST
1♣	1♠
2♠	NB

This result was claimed as a triumph for the Precision Club system, but, while it must always be satisfying to reach the correct contract after the space-consuming 2♣ opening bid, I would prefer to write this hand off as a disaster for Standard American methods. West's feeble raise to 2♠ is a good example of a player rigidly counting his points when he should be assessing the true playing strength of the hand. In view of the fact that the West hand will offer a good play for 4♠ opposite a hand as weak as

EAST
♠ A 10 8 6 3
♡ J 9 5
◇ 7 6 4
♣ 9 3

it cannot possibly be correct to make a simple raise to 2♠. I would expect any reasonably competent Acol pair to reach game on these hands by way of 1♣–1♠–3♠–4♠, or even 1♣–1♠–4♠.

THE STAGE IS YOURS

(5) Don't be tempted to switch to the Weak Two Bids which are fashionable these days—my advice is to stick to the traditional Acol structure of two openings.

While I can see that the Weak Two Bid might work well in certain circumstances, particularly when it is made on the right kind of hand, I personally would not dream of switching from the traditionally strong Acol Two—which is forcing for one round and which guarantees at least eight playing tricks plus good honour trick strength.

The principal advantages of Acol Twos are (a) that they make powerful two-suited hands relatively easy to bid, and (b) that they simplify the bidding of games and slams. As an example of this second point, here is a hand from the 1978 World Pairs Olympiad in New Orleans, in which I played with the young British star Miss Nicola Gardener.

WEST	EAST
♠ A 9	♠ J 8 3
♡ K Q J 10 9 6 4 2	♡ A 8 7 3
◇ K 7	◇ A 10 9 4
♣ 4	♣ A J

We bid to the best contract by the following route:

WEST	EAST
2♡	3♡ (1)
4NT	5♠
5NT	6♣
6NT (2)	NB

(1) An immediate raise of an Acol Two Bid shows trump support and at least one first-round control.
(2) Once my Blackwood enquiries revealed that Nicola held three aces and no kings, it was a simple matter to play in the top-scoring no trump slam.

A tense moment during a House of Commons – House of Lords match. The author, seated in the background, reviews the state of play.

36

The complete structure of opening two bids in the Acol system uses 2◇, 2♡ and 2♠ as strong, natural openings, forcing for at least one round, and uses 2♣ as an artificial strength-showing bid, forcing to game unless the auction commences 2♣–2◇–2NT. I personally prefer to play the Acol 2♣ bid in conjunction with CAB ace-showing responses, and I have come across numerous hands on which this method considerably simplifies game and slam bidding. Here is a recent example:

WEST	EAST
♠ A 10 6	♠ K 8 3
♡ K	♡ A Q 8 2
◇ A K 4	◇ 2
♣ A K J 10 9 5	♣ Q 7 6 3 2

My partner and I reached the correct contract in no time at all.

WEST	EAST
2♣	2♡ (1)
3♣	4♣
4NT (2)	5◇
5NT (3)	6♡
7NT (4)	NB

(1) Showing ♡A and no other ace.
(2) Since the precise ace holding has already been established by the initial response to 2♣, 4NT in a sequence of this kind asks for kings.
(3) Asking for queens.
(4) Unless partner's hand contained the doubleton ♡A–Q, I could count thirteen tricks at this point, and I decided to take a very slight risk and go for the top-scoring no trump slam.

As it happened, 7NT bid and made gave us an extremely good score on the board. Four pairs had reached 7NT, two played in 7♣, and the remainder failed to proceed beyond the six level. As you will have noticed, the additional bidding place released by the CAB system of responses to 2♣ made matters relatively simple for me on this occasion.

(6) *If you are contemplating a pre-emptive opening bid, try to make sure that you are pre-empting your opponents and not your partner.*

Pre-emptive opening bids almost warrant a special chapter of their own, for it is difficult to formulate a sensible set of rules to follow without introducing a number of controversial points on which even expert players would disagree. The fact of the matter is that everyone has his own individual approach to pre-empts, and it is only possible for me to set out a few general principles to guide you through doubtful situations.

The first principle to follow is probably the most important. If you are contemplating a pre-emptive opening of three, four or five in first or second position, remember that you will be shutting out your partner as well as the opponents. He may not be at all amused if he was planning to open anything up to 2♣ and finds himself pre-empted by his own partner. For this reason, pre-emptive bids in the first two positions should be well up to strength, just in case it is your partner who is on the receiving end.

I once received a charming letter from a reader who told me that a major crisis had developed in his married life because he had opened 3◇ as dealer on:

```
♠ 7
♡ 4
◇ J 10 9 8 6 5 4 2
♣ J 6 3
```

On this occasion, I had to sympathise with his wife. To pre-empt on this kind of hand before your partner has passed means in effect that you have taken a unilateral decision that the vast majority of the remaining 38 points are held by your opponents.

The second basic principle of pre-emptive bidding is that you should not expect to lose more than 300 points if you are doubled and find your partner with a completely unsuitable hand; this is the so-called Culbertson Rule of Two and Three. The late Kenneth Konstam used to advocate the principle that you should never expect to go more than two down doubled on a pre-emptive bid, but I think that your expectation of tricks should vary with the vulnerability. Let us look at some hands which qualify for a pre-emptive opening in first position at favourable vulnerability:

```
♠ K J 10 9 8 7 4      ♠ Q                  ♠ 5
♡ 7                   ♡ Q J 10 9 7 4 3     ♡ 4
◇ K 8 2               ◇ Q J 10 6           ◇ K J 9 8 6 5 4
♣ J 4                 ♣ 7                  ♣ Q J 9 6
     Open 3♠               Open 3♡                Open 3◇
```

If you are vulnerable against non-vulnerable opponents, your hand should be something like

```
♠ A Q J 9 8 6 4        ♠ J
♡ Q 7                  ♡ K J 10 9 6 5 2
◇ 10 5 2               ◇ A 7 3
♣ Q                    ♣ 6 4

     Open 3♠                Open 3♡
```

As you will see, these last two hands contain fair defensive values, and it is therefore essential that you get the right opening lead if your left-hand opponent becomes the declarer.

The example hands shown above give you some idea of my personal taste in pre-emptive openings, but I must confess that I could easily open them on Monday and pass them on Tuesday. Whether or not I decide to pre-empt on a certain hand will depend on who my partner is, on who my opponents are, and on the type of competition I am playing in. In a large pairs event, I try to do what most players are likely to do on my hand, hoping to achieve an average unless my opponents contrive to play poorly and give me a better score.

THE STAGE IS YOURS

We have been talking so far about pre-emptive opening bids in first and second position. If you are in third position after partner has passed, of course, almost anything goes in the way of pre-empts, and there is no longer any need to wait for a text-book hand to come along. Third-in-hand pre-empts often have the desired effect of pushing the opponents to an excessively high level and forcing them to make important guesses in the limited bidding space which remains available for them. For example:

♠ K J 10 8 7 4	♠ K 8 3	♠ 9 7 5 3
♡ 6 3	♡ 5	♡ K J 9 8 6 5
◇ Q 9 4 2	◇ A Q J 7 4 3	◇ K 8
♣ 7	♣ J 4 2	♣ 5
HAND A	HAND B	HAND C

These hands are completely different in nature, but my view is that they all qualify for a pre-emptive three opening in third position. 3♠ will clearly make life difficult for the opponents on Hand A, and the fact that you have reasonable values on Hand B makes it quite likely that an opening bid of 3◇ will cause the enemy to overstretch slightly and topple over.

THE STAGE IS YOURS

I actually held Hand C above in the recent Caransa Tournament, and I have to confess that, despite all my sound advice to you earlier in this section, I opened 3♡ in *first* position, before my partner had had an opportunity to bid. My only excuse is that our opponents were vulnerable and we were not. This was the complete deal:

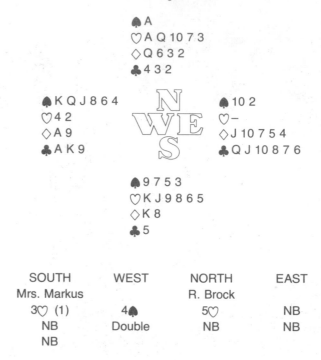

```
              ♠ A
              ♡ A Q 10 7 3
              ◇ Q 6 3 2
              ♣ 4 3 2

♠ K Q J 8 6 4              ♠ 10 2
♡ 4 2                     ♡ –
◇ A 9                     ◇ J 10 7 5 4
♣ A K 9                   ♣ Q J 10 8 7 6

              ♠ 9 7 5 3
              ♡ K J 9 8 6 5
              ◇ K 8
              ♣ 5
```

SOUTH	WEST	NORTH	EAST
Mrs. Markus		R. Brock	
3♡ (1)	4♠	5♡	NB
NB	Double	NB	NB
NB			

(1) As you can see, I do not subscribe to the theory that you should not pre-empt if you have four cards in an unbid major suit. I have found from experience that 6-4-2-1 and 7-2-2-2 hands are generally of little use in defence, and I always like to make a pre-emptive opening on hands with those shapes.

I had very little difficulty in making the requisite tricks in 5♡ doubled and, since our team-mates had bid and made 4♠ without interference at the other table, this brought in a substantial gain for my team. It is interesting to note that ten tricks are the limit in spades on the East-West hands: if West ruffs two hearts in dummy, he will lose two spade tricks and one diamond.

A pre-emptive bid at the four or five level may be based on quite a good hand if you decide to make it difficult for the other side to find its best spot. Such a bid may foil the opponents, and it will very rarely irritate your partner.

```
              ♠ K Q J 10 8 7 6 4
              ♡ –
              ◇ K Q 10 9
              ♣ 8
```

In a sense, this three-loser hand qualifies for a strength-showing opening bid. At the table, however, 4♠ is by far the best practical shot. Since the other three players hold thirteen hearts and twelve clubs between them, it is quite likely that the opponents will have anything ranging from a cheap sacrifice to a makeable slam; to deprive them of several rounds of bidding must therefore stand to gain points in the long run.

(7) *If you have already passed once, don't respond in a weak or short suit—you may be left to play in it.*

It is important to remember that you cannot stick rigidly to your normal style of constructive bidding once you have passed originally. If partner has opened on modest values, he will be keen to drop the bidding as soon as possible. This may persuade him to pass your response whenever he has anything remotely resembling adequate trump support, for example Q-x or x-x-x, and it makes it most inadvisable to respond in a weak suit after an initial pass.

Consider this hand:

NORTH	NORTH	EAST	SOUTH	WEST
♠J 5 4 2	NB	NB	1◇	NB
♡J 3	?			
◇Q 4 2				
♣A 9 7 5				

The normal response on this holding is the approach-forcing bid of 1♠, showing a four-card or longer spade suit and waiting for partner to describe his hand further. After your original pass, however, a simple change of suit response will no longer be forcing, and it would be most unwise to introduce such a weak suit when there is a distinct possibility of your being left to play in it. The most practical response in the situation set out above is a straightforward raise to 2◇.

The corollary to the above principle is that provided you have a good suit, you can make a two-level response on rather fewer values if you have passed originally. For example:

NORTH	NORTH	EAST	SOUTH	WEST
♠2	NB	NB	1♠	NB
♡Q 4	?			
◇K J 10 8 6 5				
♣9 8 7 3				

In normal circumstances, this hand would not be strong enough to respond in a new suit at the two level and, much as I hate it, I would probably make the unnatural response of 1NT. Now that you have passed originally, however, it is quite likely that partner is intending to pass over any simple response from you, and 2◇ becomes the most practical bid you can make.

THE STAGE IS YOURS

(8) *Don't restrict yourself by having a too rigid set of requirements for a two-level response in a new suit; certain responding hands call for a more flexible treatment.*

I came across an excellent example in support of this general philosophy of bidding just recently, when I was playing rubber bridge in partnership with one of the finest players in the country. He always expects at least ten high-card points for a change-of-suit response at the two level, and this accounts for the inelegant contract reached on the following deal.

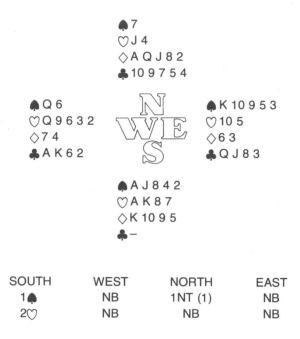

	♠ 7	
	♡ J 4	
	◇ A Q J 8 2	
	♣ 10 9 7 5 4	
♠ Q 6		♠ K 10 9 5 3
♡ Q 9 6 3 2		♡ 10 5
◇ 7 4		◇ 6 3
♣ A K 6 2		♣ Q J 8 3
	♠ A J 8 4 2	
	♡ A K 8 7	
	◇ K 10 9 5	
	♣ –	

SOUTH	WEST	NORTH	EAST
1♠	NB	1NT (1)	NB
2♡	NB	NB	NB

(1) Since I was a long way short of the ten points which my partner would expect from a response of 2♣ or 2◇, I felt obliged to make the unnatural response of 1NT.

My partner succeeded in making eleven tricks in his ridiculous contract of 2♡, but he was kind enough to remark that my bidding was perfectly correct. Alas, I did not return the compliment. In my view, South should have bid 2◇ and not 2♡ over my 1NT response, thereby keeping alive the chance of finding a fit in either red suit.

Basically, of course, our bidding disaster was caused by the fact that I was compelled to make a completely unnatural bid of 1NT on a hand which was quite unsuitable for no trump purposes, but which would play well in a suit. In future, I shall add on a point or two for distributional values on a hand of this kind, so that I can justify a natural suit response at the two level.

As you may already have guessed, rigidity is one of my pet hates in bridge. I must have a certain amount of freedom to stray slightly from the orthodox rules, which only really exist to help players of average standard and below. To my mind, the true expert must be permitted to take a few liberties when there is no other way out.

The Opponents Intervene

Tips on Bidding in a Contested Auction

THE OPPONENTS INTERVENE

When the vulnerability is in your favour, don't be afraid of overcalling at the one level on almost anything.

It seems to me that you have everything to gain by making light overcalls at the one level when you are not vulnerable against vulnerable opponents. It may be possible for you to engineer a profitable sacrifice, and you will find that you can interfere with the opponents' bidding machinery with very little risk: even if you are doubled and defeated, it will not be easy for the enemy to collect a large enough penalty to compensate them for the loss of their vulnerable game.

The following hand from a recent tournament provides a good example of my individual style in this matter. North dealt with East-West vulnerable.

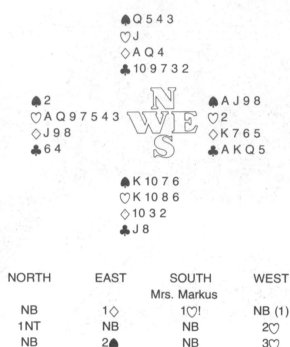

NORTH	EAST	SOUTH	WEST
		Mrs. Markus	
NB	1◇	1♡!	NB (1)
1NT	NB	NB	2♡
NB	2♠	NB	3♡
NB	NB	NB	

(1) East-West were playing "Sputnik" doubles. A double by West in this position, even at the one level, would have been for a take-out, not for penalties. While I can see that Sputnik doubles can be useful in certain circumstances, particularly when partner opens 1♣ and the next player overcalls 1♠, there seems little point in playing them when the intervening overcall has not taken up any bidding space.

As it happened, 4♡ could not be defeated on the East-West hands, but West had to play carefully to make ten tricks. He won the opening club lead in dummy and successfully finessed ♡Q. He then crossed to ♠A, ruffed a spade, and played two more top clubs. I ruffed with ♡10, but declarer discarded a losing diamond and thereby restricted his losers to two trump tricks and ◇A.

It gave me considerable satisfaction to have talked my opponents out of their vulnerable game. I enjoy playing an adventurous game of this nature and, while I cannot truthfully claim that I am always successful, I would be most reluctant to change my style. In fact, I only alter my methods if I am facing a partner who absolutely insists on a more orthodox approach.

The freedom which it gives me is one of the principal reasons why I enjoy playing rubber bridge so much, provided that I am playing at a stake which I can afford. I have always been a winning player at rubber bridge, even though I rarely hold consistently good cards; I am sure that this is partly because I look upon a poor hand as a challenge and do my utmost to get the best possible result on it. When it comes to competitive bridge, I become a little more conservative and a little more reliable in my bidding style. However, I can never be described as a coward at the bridge table, and I often feel that I have a sort of sixth sense which protects me when I am contemplating a daring, unsound bid.

Don't be frightened of bidding over a weak no trump when you are not vulnerable; if you are vulnerable, however, you must treat it with a certain amount of respect.

I have never been a great admirer of the weak no trump. It is very little help in a constructive auction, and it often results in the hand being played in the wrong denomination, particularly at the part-score level. Moreover, the fact that the opener's hand is limited and known to be fairly weak makes him extremely vulnerable to a penalty double; in my view, this makes it foolhardy to use the weak no trump when you are vulnerable, especially for money or for i.m.p. The only advantages of the weak no trump are that it makes certain balanced hands easy to bid, and that it occasionally makes it difficult for the opponents to get into the bidding.

THE OPPONENTS INTERVENE

The secret of playing against the weak no trump is not to be afraid of it and to intervene as often as you can, particularly when you are not vulnerable. The best method of entering the auction is often by way of a double. This is by definition penalty orientated, but my view is that the doubler's partner should always feel free to remove the double if his side is not vulnerable. For example, I am not convinced that South should have passed my double on the following hand, dealt by West at love all.

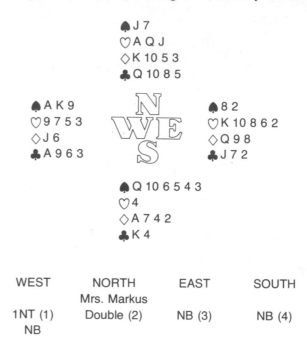

WEST	NORTH	EAST	SOUTH
	Mrs. Markus		
1NT (1)	Double (2)	NB (3)	NB (4)
NB			

(1) The weak no trump. Some partnerships have now lowered their requirements for a 1NT opening still further: to 10–12 points. I would love to challenge them to a money match.
(2) My double on a minimum opening hand gives you some idea of the contempt with which I regard the weak 1NT.
(3) This was a strange pass. With such a poor hand, East should surely have converted to 2♡.
(4) Since partner is not likely to find an opening spade lead against 1NT doubled, there is a lot to be said for seeking a game in spades on the South hand.

I led ◇3 against 1NT doubled, and declarer won the third round of diamonds with dummy's queen, discarding a small club from hand. He crossed to hand with ♠A and led a heart to my queen and dummy's king. I won the second round of hearts with ♡J and cashed ◇10, leaving the position seen in Fig. I.

I now switched to ♣10 to ♣J, ♣K and ♣A, and declarer was held to five tricks when I was able to win the next heart and cash three more club tricks. West should, of course, not cover with ♣J in the diagram position. If he ducks in dummy and captures my ♣10 with the ace, he blocks the club suit and can establish two heart tricks in dummy to land his contract.

(Fig. I)

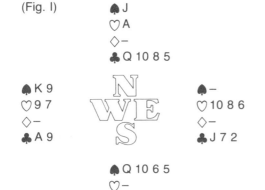

While +300 was a perfectly satisfactory score for us on the above hand, my partner would almost certainly have made 4♠ if he had elected to remove my double. The key play would be to lead ♣4 towards dummy at a fairly early stage. If West goes up with ♣A, declarer has three club tricks and can discard his two losing diamonds; and if West ducks the club, dummy's ♣Q wins and South can ruff out East's ♡K to establish a discard for his ♣K, thereby restricting his losers to two spades and one diamond.

A double of a 1NT opening bid when you are vulnerable is strictly for penalties, and partner should pass even if he has a very weak hand; for one thing, it might be cheaper to allow the opponents to make +180 or +280 in 1NT doubled than to attempt a rescue and go down doubled and vulnerable on your cards. This does, of course, mean that you must have a correspondingly stronger hand to double 1NT when you are vulnerable.

There are some hands on which you are *too* strong to double 1NT, either because you are afraid that your partner might not be able to pass your double, which might arise when the opponents are vulnerable and you are not, or because the resulting penalty might not be sufficient, which might arise if the vulnerabilities are reversed. I took this view on the following hand from a recent teams event (Fig. II); West dealt with North-South vulnerable.

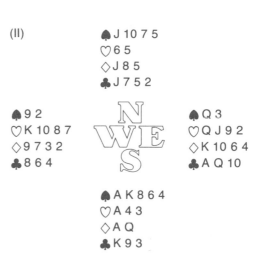

WEST	NORTH	EAST	SOUTH
			Mrs. Markus
NB	NB	1NT	3NT (1)
NB	NB	NB	

(1) This was a difficult decision. I was frightened that even if my partner left a double in, which was by no means certain, we might have a struggle to collect an adequate penalty if we could make a vulnerable game on the North-South cards. I therefore decided to go for the maximum and bid the game myself, hoping that my partner would hold a useful card or two. As you can see, I am not a player who likes to sit back and wait for things to happen.

West found the best lead of ♡7, but nothing could stop me from making nine tricks when the spades broke 2–2: I had five spades, one heart, two diamonds and one club. As the cards lay, I could also have made 4♠, but +600 was a very satisfactory score. The opponents holding the North-South cards at the other table achieved only +140 in a spade part-score.

You may think that I was lucky to find my partner with such a suitable hand on the above deal. Perhaps I was, but my whole psychology at bridge is based on courage. Like many people who are daring in real life, I occasionally pay dearly for my optimism. However, I must follow my principles and, provided that I stick to them unwaveringly, I am convinced that my successes will heavily outweigh my failures.

THE OPPONENTS INTERVENE

Don't try to trap your opponents by not intervening on a good hand: you will often only succeed in trapping your own side.

I am not a member of the Hudson Bay Association. In other words, I do not believe in trapping: if the opponents open the bidding and I have a good hand, I like to get into the auction. The following hand from a recent International Pairs Tournament shows you why I think the way I do on the subject. East dealt with North-South vulnerable.

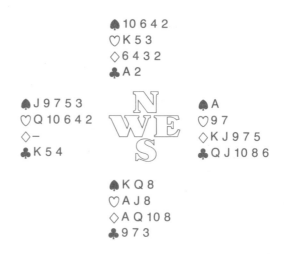

This was the bidding at one table:

EAST	SOUTH	WEST	NORTH
1◇	NB (1)	1♠	NB
2♣	NB (2)	NB	NB

(1) A trap pass, hoping that East-West would hurtle onwards to their own destruction.
(2) Things are already failing to turn out the way South wanted.

2♣ went one down, but +50 proved to be an inadequate score for North-South. When I held the South hand, I bid 1NT over East's 1◇ opening and that became the final contract. West led a spade, and East won with ♠A and switched to ♣Q. I won the second club in dummy and played a diamond to my ◇8. I then cashed ♠K-Q and crossed to dummy with ♡K to finesse ◇10. West did well by discarding ♣K on this trick, for I could otherwise have thrown him in with it and forced him to lead a heart into my tenace. As it was, I was able to cash ♡A and exit with a club, forcing East to cash his club tricks and then give me two more tricks in diamonds. Two spades, two hearts, four diamonds and one club gave me nine tricks and a good match-point score on the board.

Don't miss an opportunity of doubling the opponents when you can tell from the bidding that the cards are lying very badly for them.

The ability to double at the right time is one of the distinguishing marks of an expert player. At a high level, I have found from experience that the most profitable doubles occur when (a) both the opponents' hands are known to be limited and (b) the cards are lying badly or the suits breaking poorly for the opponents, or both.

My double produced an unexpected windfall on the following hand, dealt by East at game all.

```
                    ♠ 10 6 4 3
                    ♡ 4 2
                    ◇ 2
                    ♣ A J 7 6 5 2

    ♠ Q                           ♠ K J 9 8
    ♡ 8 7 3          N            ♡ K 10 9 5
    ◇ Q 10 8 7 5   W   E          ◇ A J 6 3
    ♣ K Q 9 3        S            ♣ 10

                    ♠ A 7 5 2
                    ♡ A Q J 6
                    ◇ K 9 4
                    ♣ 8 4
```

It is not often that I make four consecutive passes in one auction.

EAST	SOUTH	WEST	NORTH
	Mrs. Markus		
1♡	NB	2◇	NB
3◇	NB	3♡	NB
3♠	NB	3NT	NB
4◇	NB	5◇	NB
NB	Double (1)	NB	NB
NB			

(1) Once West had shown three-card support for hearts, I felt certain that I had three heart tricks in defence. I also hoped that my double would enable my partner to find an opening heart lead. 5◇ doubled went four down after the ♡4 opening lead — +1100.

The opponents were rather unlucky in that they each held a lot of wasted values, and I expect that our silence throughout the auction caused them to overvalue their hands.

As you can see, I sometimes keep silent on good hands to quite good effect, while on other hands I like to intervene on slender values. My judgement usually guides me, and I have found that experience is an excellent teacher. If you try to follow my methods and find that they do not suit you, don't blame me: I can only suggest that you develop your own ideas and then stick to them. The important point is that you should not change your direction too often. Don't overbid on Monday and hold back on Tuesday, or your partner will not know what to expect.

THE OPPONENTS INTERVENE

The "Unusual No Trump" can be a very effective weapon, but it must be handled carefully if it is to produce good results.

The so-called "Unusual No Trump" has grown considerably in recent years. It was originally a purely defensive weapon, aimed at pre-empting the opponents and suggesting a possible sacrifice, but its uses have now been expanded to such an extent that it can sometimes be employed as a constructive manoeuvre by the opening side. For example:

SOUTH	NORTH	EAST	SOUTH	WEST
♠ 7 4 2	2♢	2♠	NB	4♠
♡ J 9 7 5 4	4NT	NB	?	
♢ 6				
♣ Q 10 6 3				

North's bid of 4NT in this situation can scarcely be Blackwood, and it must therefore be the "Unusual No Trump", asking you to choose between two suits. North's principal suit is known to be diamonds and, since he could have bid 5♣ over 4♠ without raising the level of the bidding unnecessarily, the inference is that his second suit is hearts. Your correct bid over 4NT is therefore 5♡, and you can confidently expect this kind of hand to go down as dummy: ♠x ♡ A-K-x-x ♢A-K-J-x-x-x ♣ A-x.

Unusual Principles

	♠ A	
	♡ J 4	
	♢ A Q 10 9 5	
	♣ A Q 9 6 3	
♠ J 8 6 4	N	♠ K 7 5
♡ K 7	W E	♡ A Q 10 8 6 2
♢ J 8 6 3	S	♢ 7 4 2
♣ K 10 5		♣ 7
	♠ Q 10 9 3 2	
	♡ 9 5 3	
	♢ K	
	♣ J 8 4 2	

The principal use of the Unusual No Trump is still to show long suits in defence. These are normally the minor suits, but the Unusual No Trump can be used to show length in any two suits if the opponents have bid the other two. If it is only employed on suitable hands, containing at least 5-5 in the two relevant suits, the Unusual No Trump can be extremely effective. I remember, for example, a deal from the Great Britain v. Ireland match in Turin in 1960. East dealt with North-South vulnerable.

EAST	SOUTH	WEST	NORTH
	Mrs. Markus		Mrs. Whittaker
1♡	NB	1NT	2NT
NB	3♣	NB	4♣
NB	5♣	NB	NB
NB			

The defence began with three rounds of hearts, and I ruffed in dummy, crossed to hand with ♢K and led ♣J. West covered with ♣K, and I won with dummy's ♣A. Since East was known to have six hearts and at least three spades (four unless West had declined to bid a four-card spade suit in response to 1♡), she had four minor suit cards at most. There were seven diamonds and four clubs in the East-West hands, and I decided that the odds favoured East holding two or three diamonds and one club rather than one or two diamonds and two clubs. I therefore crossed back to hand by ruffing a diamond and led a small club, successfully finessing dummy's ♣9. That was +600 and a useful swing to Great Britain; the Irish North-South pair at the other table made exactly ten tricks in their contract of 4♣.

Accept the fact that a certain number of pre-empts will work out well against you—that is why everyone uses pre-emptive bids.

Pre-emptive bids have existed for a great number of years, and they are used just as often as ever at the present time. There is, therefore, no reason to believe that you will ever be able to get away from pre-empts entirely, and my view is that you simply have to accept this and resign yourself to the fact that you will not be able to deal satisfactorily with every single pre-emptive opening by the opponents. Some pre-empts work; that is why people use pre-empts.

Over the years, I have experimented with all the recognised methods of dealing with pre-empts. None of them works in every situation, and I have yet to find a more satisfactory method than the common-or-garden take-out double. The use of a double to show a strong hand and to ask partner to describe his holding has two principal advantages over all other take-out conventions: (a) it leaves the maximum possible bidding space available for the defending side; and (b) it leaves 3NT and all suit bids over pre-empts for use in a natural sense.

The weakness of my favourite defence to weak three-bids is that I occasionally miss a profitable penalty when I have a good holding in trumps *over* the opening bidder. However, I console myself when that happens by remembering that there is no method which acts as a complete remedy over opposing pre-empts. If you do happen to come across one, please let me know.

Dealing with pre-empts

If you are in doubt whether or not to enter the auction over an opposing pre-empt, remember that you must have a good hand to enter the auction at the three level. It is important not to allow yourself to be pre-empted by your opponents into a disaster, and I have always found that it pays to take your medicine and pass if you are in any doubt: you may miss the occasional game or slam through failing to get into the bidding, but it will pay you in the long run to cut your losses and settle for a modest plus score. Nobody knows more than I do how difficult it can be to pass, but you must make sure that you have sufficient values before you set the ball rolling at a high level.

Rixi Markus with friends pause for a moment during a non-competitive game. Among the group are Henri Shoucair on the left, and the Comte de Henricourt on the right.

THE OPPONENTS INTERVENE

While an opposing pre-empt can be a devastating weapon, it can also serve as a warning that the suits are going to break badly.

If you are wondering how high to go after a weak three opening by one of your opponents, heed the gipsy's warning: the suits will probably not break kindly for you, and it might therefore pay to keep a little in reserve.

The ringing of the warning bells might also assist you in the play of the hand. For example, consider this hand from the 1978 Caransa Team Event.

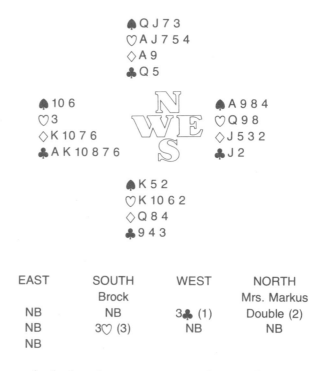

	EAST	SOUTH	WEST	NORTH
		Brock		Mrs. Markus
	NB	NB	3♣ (1)	Double (2)
	NB	3♡ (3)	NB	NB
	NB			

(1) As we saw in the last chapter, a pre-emptive opening based on quite reasonable values can often work out well.

(2) A take-out double.

(3) My partner had a lot to spare for his simple bid of 3♡, but he was conscious of his unpromising 4-3-3-3 distribution and of the fact that it often pays to keep a little in reserve when all the suits are likely to break badly.

In normal circumstances, North-South would probably have reached 4♡ and complained about their ill-fortune when it proved impossible to make. However, Raymond Brock heeded the warnings after West's opening three-bid, and he played well to make nine tricks in hearts.

West began by leading three rounds of clubs against 3♡. If declarer ruffs the third club in dummy, he is bound to lose five tricks: one spade, one heart, one diamond and two clubs. Brock found the neat solution of discarding dummy's diamond loser on the third round of clubs. He was then able to finesse East for ♡Q and restrict his losers to four: three clubs and ♠A.

The Play
Tips on the Play of the Hand

THE PLAY

I mentioned in Chapter 1 my belief that the first basic requirement of a good bridge player is an ability to count. This is particularly true in relation to dummy play, when the declarer must concentrate his entire efforts on counting: counting the cards in each suit as they are played; counting the opponents' hands and their highcard points; and counting his available tricks.

The Vital Count

This theme will reappear on several occasions throughout this chapter, in which I shall set out a number of practical tips designed to help you sharpen up your declarer play. My first tip, for example, is based entirely on the need for accurate counting.

(1) *Count your tricks, both when dummy first appears and after each new development in the play.*

This may seem an extremely elementary point, but I have always found that the most common explanation for a declarer going down in a makeable contract is that he failed to count his tricks. Here is a recent example; I was defending with the West hand when the declarer muddled the play in 4♠.

I led ◇3 against 4♠, and my partner won with ◇A and returned a second diamond to dummy's queen. This defence would appear to do very little damage to the declarer, but he still managed to go one down. He drew trumps in three rounds and cashed ◇K, discarding the losing club from dummy. He then ruffed a diamond in dummy, establishing a winning diamond in his hand, and cashed ♣A. He was now forced to lead ♡Q from dummy, and I won with ♡A and fired back a second heart to my partner's ♡10. South ruffed, cashed his long diamond and led ♣J, but I went up with ♣K and played a third heart for my partner to take the setting trick with ♡K.

If South had counted his tricks correctly, he would have come to ten, once the spades are known to be 3-2 and the diamonds no worse than 4-2. He can count five spade tricks, including one ruff in dummy, three diamonds and two clubs, and his error was to discard dummy's small club on ◇K. Declarer can afford to lose one heart, one diamond and one club, and the correct sequence of play after drawing trumps is to cash ◇K, ruff a diamond in dummy and then play ♣A and another club. In this way, ten tricks are guaranteed.

(2) *An overcall by the opponents will often make things more difficult in the bidding, but it will normally simplify matters in the play of the hand.*

If you eventually become the declarer after a contested auction, you must always bear the opponents' bidding in mind while you are playing the hand. This will often enable you to pick up a vital clue to the successful line of play.

The deal in Fig. I is a good illustration of the above principle.

The bidding may look strange, but it is easily explained.

NORTH	EAST	SOUTH	WEST
NB	NB	1◇ (1)	1♠
2♡	NB	2NT	NB
3NT	NB	NB	NB

(Fig. I)

♠ Q 8 6 4
♡ A 9 8 6 4
◇ K 8
♣ Q 3

♠ A J 9 5 3   ♠ 7
♡ J 3   ♡ K 10 7 5 2
◇ 10   ◇ Q J 7 6 5 4
♣ J 10 8 7 5   ♣ 4

♠ K 10 2
♡ Q
◇ A 9 3 2
♣ A K 9 6 2

(1) North-South were playing the Precision Club System, but South did not consider that his hand was quite worth an artificial strength-showing bid of 1♣. I am sure he was right, for the singleton ♡Q is a doubtful asset and this kind of hand may prove to be of limited use unless partner holds good values opposite.

Unaware of the true nature of South's hand, West led ♣J to dummy's ♣Q. Declarer immediately played a small heart towards his singleton queen, and East went up with ♡K and switched to ♠7.

Bearing in mind West's 1♠ overcall, declarer now knew the full distribution of the spade suit. West's opening lead and East's failure to continue the suit suggested that East was also short of clubs, and South was beginning to build up a pretty fair mental picture of the full deal. He went up with ♠K on East's spade return, and West allowed this to hold the trick.

South now played a diamond to dummy's king, felling West's singleton 10, and continued with a small diamond from dummy, ducking when East split his honours. East was already under pressure. He returned a heart to his partner's ♡J, but South won with dummy's ace and fired back ♡9. East won and found himself in the position in Fig. II.

East was now completely endplayed. South had already made four tricks, and a heart return from East would give declarer two more heart tricks and his contract. East was therefore compelled to exit with a diamond, but South finessed ◇9 and led a spade towards dummy's ♠Q to develop his ninth trick.

(II)

♠ Q 8 6
♡ 8 6
◇ –
♣ 3

♠ A J 9   ♠ –
♡ –   ♡ 7 5
◇ –   ◇ Q 7 6 5
♣ 10 8 7   ♣ –

♠ 10 2
♡ –
◇ A 9
♣ A K

The Vital Clue

This is one of those curious hands on which the declarer sets out a long way short of his contract but the defenders are completely unable to defeat him. The important point to notice is the way in which South derived the vital clue from West's overcall and then slotted in the missing pieces of the puzzle as the play developed.

THE PLAY

(3) As well as picking up important clues from the opponents' bidding, the declarer can often draw a vital inference from their failure to bid.

I cannot stress too strongly the importance of constantly remaining alert when you are the declarer. As the play develops, for example, you may be able to pick up a vital clue as to the full layout by remembering a moment of silence during the bidding.

Sit behind my chair while I replay an interesting hand which I held recently. South dealt at love all.

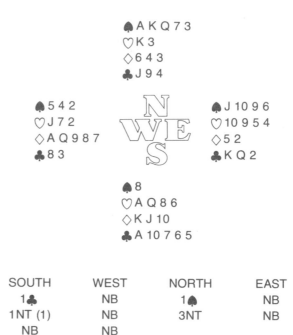

♠ A K Q 7 3
♡ K 3
◇ 6 4 3
♣ J 9 4

♠ 5 4 2
♡ J 7 2
◇ A Q 9 8 7
♣ 8 3

♠ J 10 9 6
♡ 10 9 5 4
◇ 5 2
♣ K Q 2

♠ 8
♡ A Q 8 6
◇ K J 10
♣ A 10 7 6 5

SOUTH	WEST	NORTH	EAST
1♣	NB	1♠	NB
1NT (1)	NB	3NT	NB
NB	NB		

(1) I do not normally like to rebid in no trumps when I have a singleton in my partner's suit, but there was no sensible alternative on this occasion: the hand was not strong enough for a reverse bid of 2♡, but I considered it slightly too good for a simple rebid of 2♣.

West led ◇8 to my ◇10 and I was faced with an immediate problem. If West held only four diamonds, I could afford to play on clubs. However, if West held a five-card suit, there was only one real chance for my contract. I won ◇10 and immediately returned a second diamond. This forced West to cash his four diamond tricks if he was to enjoy them at all, and East was hopelessly squeezed in the other three suits. He could throw one club in complete safety, but his second discard would automatically give me my ninth trick.

A Spectacular Play

This type of play is always an enjoyable one to find and a spectacular one to execute. More important, however, is my reason for deciding not to play on clubs. The clue came from the sequence of cards at trick one, when the play went ◇8, ◇3, ◇5, ◇10. If East's ◇5 was a sensible card, it must be either (a) a singleton, (b) the beginning of a distributional peter from 5-2 or (c) a discouraging play from 7-5 doubleton. In case (a), West would have A-Q-x-x-x-x; in cases (b) and (c) he would have A-Q-x-x-x. Since West would probably have chipped in with a non-vulnerable overcall of 1◇ if he held a good six-card suit headed by ace-queen, I reasoned that he almost certainly held a five-card suit. This made it safe to exit with a diamond at trick two.

Taking the argument one stage further, West might also have overcalled 1◇ if he held ◇AQ98x and an honour in clubs, and the likelihood that East held both club honours and would be able to push a diamond through made it dangerous to play on clubs in the normal manner. The only real hope was therefore to fire back a diamond at the second trick, and my careful counting was rewarded when nine tricks rolled in.

(4) *It is rarely correct to try to make as many tricks as possible on every hand. If you can afford to lose a trick or two, you should concentrate your energies on making sure that you do not lose more.*

The term "safety play" has acquired a number of different meanings in our bridge language. A perfect safety play is one which absolutely *guarantees* a given number of tricks from a key suit. For example:

NORTH
K Q 9 5 2

SOUTH
A 10 4 3

By leading the king first, South is certain to make all five tricks even against a 4-0 break.

Other safety plays are designed to ensure that your losses in a particular suit are restricted to a given maximum figure.

NORTH
K 9 5 4 2

SOUTH
A 10 8 3

South will often be able to make all five tricks from this holding. However, he must take special care if he only needs four tricks. In this case, to start with the ace or king will prove fatal if the wrong opponent is revealed to hold Q-J-x-x, and the safety play for four tricks is to lead a low card from either hand, intending to finesse the 9 or 10 if the next player follows with a small card.

THE PLAY

The third and probably most common variety of safety play is one which does not guarantee satisfaction but which gives declarer the best chance of making the required number of tricks—often by giving up all hope of making the maximum number. Here is a good example from a recent competition in Venice:

```
                    ♠ 7 5 4
                    ♡ A K 9 8 3
                    ◇ A Q 8
                    ♣ 7 4

  ♠ 9 6 3 2          N          ♠ Q J 10
  ♡ Q 10 6 4      W     E       ♡ J 7 2
  ◇ 6 5 4 3          S          ◇ 2
  ♣ K                           ♣ J 10 9 8 6 2

                    ♠ A K 8
                    ♡ 5
                    ◇ K J 10 9 7
                    ♣ A Q 5 3
```

You, South, become the declarer in 6◇, and West leads a small trump. As always, you count your tricks carefully, and you find that you can park your losing spade on one of dummy's top hearts. This means that a successful club finesse will almost certainly give you all thirteen tricks, for you can cash two spades, two hearts and two clubs and then make seven trump tricks by playing along cross-ruff lines.

However, the club finesse is *not* the correct play in a small slam. In 6◇, you can afford to lose one club trick as long as you make two, and the best line is to cash ♣A and then cross to dummy to lead towards your ♣Q. This succeeds whenever East has ♣K, and also caters for the additional chance of West's holding the singleton king. When ♣K drops on the first round, of course, your best play is to continue with a small club; nothing can then prevent you from collecting one club ruff in dummy as your twelfth trick. Notice that the greedy play of finessing ♣Q at trick two would be absolutely fatal as the cards actually lay.

All world champions together at Deauville, *R. Bacherich (France) M. D'Alelio (Italy) Rixi Markus and Frizi Gordon (Gt. Britain) G. Belladona* and *Y. Avarelli (Italy).*

(5) *Never give up hope if you find yourself in an appalling contract. If you need to find a certain distribution of cards in the opponents' hands in order to scramble home, assume that the required distribution exists and play accordingly.*

Even the world's best bidders occasionally reach very poor contracts. You must therefore not despair if you end up in an almost hopeless spot: you must concentrate on finding a distribution which will enable you to succeed and then plan your play of the hand accordingly.

For example, it would be difficult to recommend South's contract of 3NT on the hand in Fig. III, but he succeeded in bringing in 600 points.

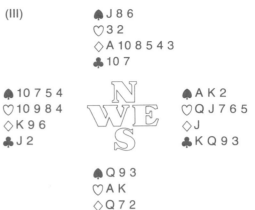

(III)

♠ J 8 6
♡ 3 2
◇ A 10 8 5 4 3
♣ 10 7

♠ 10 7 5 4　　　♠ A K 2
♡ 10 9 8 4　　　♡ Q J 7 6 5
◇ K 9 6　　　　◇ J
♣ J 2　　　　　♣ K Q 9 3

♠ Q 9 3
♡ A K
◇ Q 7 2
♣ A 8 6 5 4

SOUTH	WEST	NORTH	EAST
1♣	NB	1◇	Double
1NT	NB	2◇	2♡
3NT	NB	NB	NB

South's leap to 3NT was clearly made in the hope that his good fit in diamonds would bring in six tricks in the suit, and he must have have been extremely disappointed when he saw dummy. However, he soon realised that he had to base his hopes on making all six diamond tricks, and that there was only one distribution which would make this possible: ◇K-x-x in the West hand and the singleton jack with East.

After winning the opening heart lead, therefore, South successfully played for the only real chance of nine tricks: he led ◇Q from hand, forcing West to cover with ◇K and bringing down ◇J from East. A club to ♣A and a diamond to dummy's ◇8 followed, and it was all over.

This hand reminds me of a famous player who always used to complain if his partner started to count his points when he was a little short for his bid. "Who needs points?" he would ask. "I need tricks!"

Achieving the impossible

The hand in Fig. IV was played in rubber bridge by current British international Claude Rodrigue. He was able to achieve what at first sight appeared to be absolutely impossible.

5◇, or even 6◇, would have been a comfortable contract on the North-South cards, but Rodrigue found himself playing in 3NT from the wrong side of the table. These things happen in rubber bridge.

West led ♡J against 3NT, and East won the first trick with ♡K and returned a second heart. Rodrigue's first move was to lead ◇J from dummy, in the hope that East would be tempted into covering with K-x or Q-x. When this failed, South went up with ◇A and tried another approach. He crossed to dummy with ♠K and successfully finessed ♠J in hand—and suddenly the impossible contract became possible again. The continuation of ♠A squeezed West in three suits. He clearly could not throw a diamond, and to discard a club would enable declarer to make all four club tricks and nine tricks in all. He was therefore forced to abandon a winning heart, and this allowed Rodrigue to drive out ◇K in safety.

Never give up hope. I always believe that you will find a solution to most problems if you try hard enough.

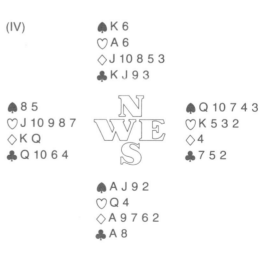

(IV)

♠ K 6
♡ A 6
◇ J 10 8 5 3
♣ K J 9 3

♠ 8 5　　　　　♠ Q 10 7 4 3
♡ J 10 9 8 7　　♡ K 5 3 2
◇ K Q　　　　　◇ 4
♣ Q 10 6 4　　　♣ 7 5 2

♠ A J 9 2
♡ Q 4
◇ A 9 7 6 2
♣ A 8

THE PLAY

(6) *Don't put all your eggs in one basket. Where you have more than one hope of making your contract, you must make certain that your sequence of play combines all available chances.*

There are many hands on which you can combine your chances in a no trump contract by playing for the drop in one suit before taking a finesse in another. The following type of situation is fairly common:

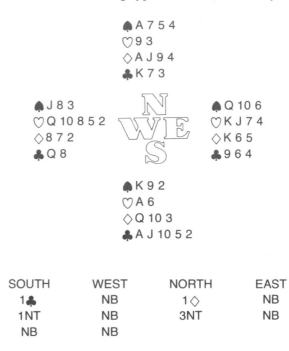

♠ A 7 5 4
♡ 9 3
◇ A J 9 4
♣ K 7 3

♠ J 8 3   ♠ Q 10 6
♡ Q 10 8 5 2   ♡ K J 7 4
◇ 8 7 2   ◇ K 6 5
♣ Q 8   ♣ 9 6 4

♠ K 9 2
♡ A 6
◇ Q 10 3
♣ A J 10 5 2

SOUTH	WEST	NORTH	EAST
1♣	NB	1◇	NB
1NT	NB	3NT	NB
NB	NB		

West leads ♡5 against 3NT, and South wins the second round with the ace. Declarer clearly needs to take the next eight tricks if he is to make his contract, and he can see that a successful finesse in either minor suit should see him home. However, he cannot take *both* finesses, for if the first one fails it will be too late to attempt the second. In order to combine his chances, therefore, South must play for the drop in one suit before finessing the other: the best plan is to cash ♣A-K in the hope of dropping ♣Q in two rounds, intending to fall back on the diamond finesse if the club suit fails to produce five tricks.

The Brazilian declarer combined his chances effectively (see Fig. V) during the Final of the Rosenblum Teams Cup at the New Orleans Olympiad in 1978. South dealt at game all.

The Polish North-South pair scored +620 in the sensible contract of 4♠. At the other table, however, one of the best pairs in the world, Chagas and Assumpcao of Brazil, reached the hair-raising contract of 3NT.

West led ♡3 to the queen and king and, although the club finesse obviously offered the main chance of nine immediate tricks, Gabriel Chagas started by leading ♠Q from the closed hand. He clearly intended to play ♠A from dummy in any case, but West could not possibly foresee this and he made the natural play of covering with ♠K. It could now cost nothing to cash ♠J before tackling the clubs, and the fall of ♠10 from East gave Brazil nine tricks without the need to resort to the club finesse. In fact, when Chagas subsequently cashed ♣A for his ninth trick, the fall of West's singleton ♣K gave him all thirteen.

(V)
♠ A J 7 4 2
♡ 6 4
◇ A
♣ Q 10 7 6 5

♠ K 5 3   ♠ 10 6
♡ A J 7 3 2   ♡ Q 10 5
◇ J 10 9 3   ◇ 8 7 6 5 4 2
♣ K   ♣ 9 2

♠ Q 9 8
♡ K 9 8
◇ K Q
♣ A J 8 4 3

Different considerations apply in a suit contract, where the best combination of plays is more likely to be to play for the drop in one suit before attempting to obtain discards on another. Consider this hand from a recent teams event:

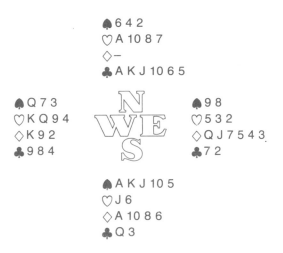

```
                    ♠ 6 4 2
                    ♡ A 10 8 7
                    ◇ -
                    ♣ A K J 10 6 5

   ♠ Q 7 3           N            ♠ 9 8
   ♡ K Q 9 4      W     E         ♡ 5 3 2
   ◇ K 9 2           S            ◇ Q J 7 5 4 3
   ♣ 9 8 4                        ♣ 7 2

                    ♠ A K J 10 5
                    ♡ J 6
                    ◇ A 10 8 6
                    ♣ Q 3
```

South became the declarer in the second-best slam contract of 6♠, and West led ♡K. The play was soon over. Declarer won the first trick with ♡A, cashed ♠A and crossed to dummy with a diamond ruff in order to finesse ♠J. One down.

In my view, the best line of play is to win ♡A and cash the two top spades. If ♠Q appears in two rounds, which is by no means a remote possibility, you are home. If spades break 3-2 and ♠Q fails to appear, you turn your attention to the club suit and hope that you can discard your losing heart without one of the first two rounds of clubs being ruffed by the defender with the third trump.

This line will only fail if the trumps are 5-0 or 4-1, or if either opponent holds ♠Q-x-x and a singleton or void in clubs, and it seems to me to be the best percentage play.

Incidentally, my partner gained 2 i.m.p. by going one down in 6♠. We should, however, have gained substantially as a result of our superior bidding, for the North-South players at the other table went two down in 7♠.

From left to right, Michael Wolach (Gt. Britain) partnered by Rita Jacobson (South African champion) playing against Leon Yallouse – George Gresh from Egypt eagerly watched by Rixi Markus.

THE PLAY

(7) *When there are problems of communications between the two hands, bear in mind the possibility of unblocking to create an extra entry—even if you risk giving an unnecessary trick to the opponents.*

Some of the most difficult hands to play are those where there is either a lack of communication between the two hands or a pronounced shortage of entries to one of them. Here is an interesting hand which was played by Peter Jay, at the time our Ambassador in Washington. He had to make 3NT on the following deal:

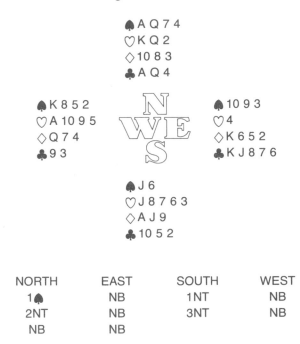

NORTH	EAST	SOUTH	WEST
1♠	NB	1NT	NB
2NT	NB	3NT	NB
NB	NB		

West led ♡10 against 3NT, and dummy's ♡K held the first trick. Peter Jay immediately played a small diamond to the nine, and West won with the queen and switched to ♣9, ducked to East's ♣J. East returned a second diamond, and Jay successfully finessed ◇J and led ♡8 towards dummy's ♡Q.

In an effort to cut declarer off from his heart suit, West went up with ♡A and fired back another diamond, removing South's last entry. However, Jay had foreseen the danger of being blocked in dummy, and he threw dummy's ♡Q under West's ace. The position after the third round of diamonds is seen in Fig. VI.

South's unblocking play had, of course, established an additional heart trick for West, but it proved to be in a good cause when declarer read the end position correctly. He cashed ♣A and threw West in by playing ♡J and another heart. West was forced to return a spade, and South won with ♠J, cashed his winning heart and finessed dummy's ♠Q for his ninth trick.

This was a well-played hand, but West was a little sleepy in the end game. After being thrown in with ♡9, he should switch to ♠K! This dramatic play restricts South to two spade tricks—eight tricks in all.

(VI)

An unusual unblocking play on the following hand from rubber bridge won US star Harold Ogust the Charles Solomon "Hand of the Year" award in 1977. South dealt at game all.

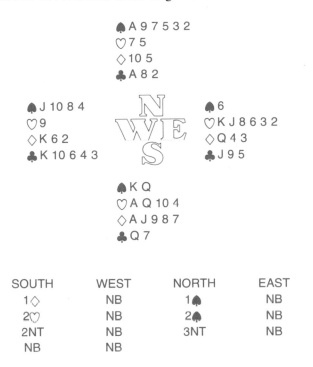

♠A 9 7 5 3 2
♡7 5
◇10 5
♣A 8 2

♠J 10 8 4
♡9
◇K 6 2
♣K 10 6 4 3

♠6
♡K J 8 6 3 2
◇Q 4 3
♣J 9 5

♠K Q
♡A Q 10 4
◇A J 9 8 7
♣Q 7

SOUTH	WEST	NORTH	EAST
1◇	NB	1♠	NB
2♡	NB	2♠	NB
2NT	NB	3NT	NB
NB	NB		

West led ♣4, and South captured East's ♣J with ♣Q.

Counting his certain tricks, Ogust could see that if spades were breaking 3-2, he had ten readily available. The problem was to find an alternative source of tricks if the adverse spades were divided 4-1. This obviously involved bringing home South's diamond suit, and this in turn meant making the most of the few entries to dummy.

After winning the first trick with ♣Q, Ogust cashed ♠K and led ♠Q from hand. When West followed to the second round of spades, South overtook with the ace in dummy. If East had also followed suit, declarer would have conceded a spade and re-entered dummy with ♣A to make three more spade tricks. This line would have presented the defenders with a spade trick which was not rightfully theirs, but it would also have given declarer enough tricks for his vulnerable game.

When East showed out on the second round, Ogust had to abandon the spade suit. However, he now had the lead where he wanted it, and he was able to turn his attention to diamonds. He led ◇10 from dummy and, with ♣A remaining in dummy as an entry for a second diamond finesse, nothing could prevent declarer from making two spades, one heart, four diamonds and two clubs—nine tricks in all.

THE PLAY

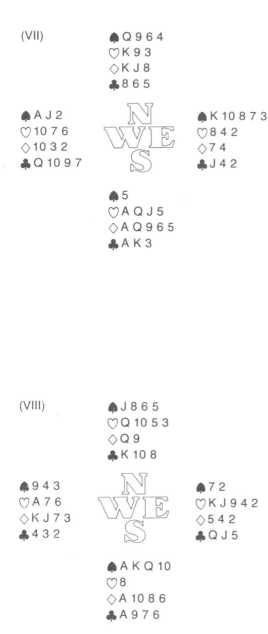

(VII)
```
                ♠ Q 9 6 4
                ♡ K 9 3
                ◇ K J 8
                ♣ 8 6 5
♠ A J 2                          ♠ K 10 8 7 3
♡ 10 7 6                         ♡ 8 4 2
◇ 10 3 2                         ◇ 7 4
♣ Q 10 9 7                       ♣ J 4 2
                ♠ 5
                ♡ A Q J 5
                ◇ A Q 9 6 5
                ♣ A K 3
```

(VIII)
```
                ♠ J 8 6 5
                ♡ Q 10 5 3
                ◇ Q 9
                ♣ K 10 8
♠ 9 4 3                          ♠ 7 2
♡ A 7 6                          ♡ K J 9 4 2
◇ K J 7 3                        ◇ 5 4 2
♣ 4 3 2                          ♣ Q J 5
                ♠ A K Q 10
                ♡ 8
                ◇ A 10 8 6
                ♣ A 9 7 6
```

(8) *If you are short of tricks in a suit contract, you should consider whether you can make more ruffing tricks by making dummy the master hand.*

The normal approach in a suit contract is to look for extra tricks by ruffing in the hand with the shorter trump holding. On certain hands, you will find it more productive to ruff with the long trumps and then draw trumps with the shorter holding. Such play is known as a Dummy Reversal.

Here, in Fig. VII, is a perfect example of a Dummy Reversal by Mrs. Joan Durran, one of the few British ladies to win an Olympic Gold Medal. She was at the wheel in 6◇.

West led ♠A and ♠J, ruffed by South. In view of her third-round club loser, Mrs. Durran decided that her best chance lay in a Dummy Reversal. Having ruffed the second spade, she led ♡5 and finessed dummy's ♡9 when the unsuspecting West played small. When ♡9 held, she ruffed a spade, crossed to ♡K and ruffed dummy's last spade with ◇A. ◇Q and a small diamond to dummy now enabled her to draw the outstanding trumps and cash ♡A-Q and ♣A-K for her contract.

The more observant among you will have noticed that West could have defeated the contract by inserting ♡10 on the first round of the suit; this would have denied South the vital extra entry to dummy. This bears out what I have often said in the past: many contracts can be made, and most contracts can be defeated.

(9) *Even when a hand looks very straightforward, treat it with the same care as you would a problem hand.*

As I remarked a little earlier, most contracts can be defeated if you give your opponents the chance. Even in an apparently simple contract, therefore, you must concentrate on not giving the opponents an opportunity to shape your destiny.

Fig. VIII shows the kind of hand which I have in mind.

SOUTH	WEST	NORTH	EAST
1◇	NB	1♡	NB
1♠	NB	2♠	NB
4♠	NB	NB	NB

West led ♣2 against 4♠, and declarer captured East's ♣J with ♣A. After this helpful lead, declarer thought that 4♠ was a simple contract, and he confidently drew trumps in three rounds and finessed dummy's ♣10. Disaster. To South's surprise and consternation, East won with ♣Q and switched to a diamond to West's ◇K. ♡A and another heart from West now removed South's last trump, and he could only get back to his hand to make the long club by overtaking dummy's ◇Q. One down.

My suggested line of play in 4♠ is to win ♣A and immediately lead a small diamond towards dummy's ◇Q. As long as you can either develop a second diamond trick or ruff two diamonds in dummy you should make ten tricks even if the adverse spades are divided 4-1.

(10) *If the defenders are about to embark on a forcing game, consider the possibility of not drawing trumps—to leave just one trump in dummy may be enough to maintain control.*

I was glad that my left-hand opponent had not read this tip before he played the following hand in a recent pairs tournament. West dealt at game all.

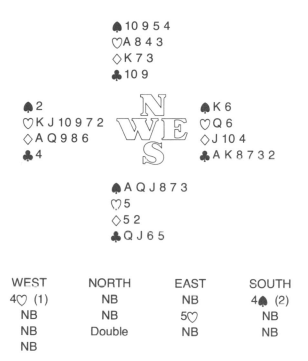

WEST	NORTH	EAST	SOUTH
4♡ (1)	NB	NB	4♠ (2)
NB	NB	5♡	NB
NB	Double	NB	NB
NB			

(1) Not everyone would agree with a pre-emptive opening on this hand, but aggressive tactics often succeed in the pairs game. An opening bid of this kind might make it difficult for the opponents to get together and might attract a favourable lead if you buy the contract; furthermore, 4♡ will very rarely be doubled.

(2) It takes more than a four-level pre-empt to keep me out of the auction on a hand like this.

North led ♠10, and I captured ♠K with my ace and returned a second spade, ruffed by declarer. West played a heart to dummy's ♡Q and continued with a second round of trumps. My partner won with ♡A and returned another spade, reducing declarer to equal length in trumps. West now banked everything on the diamond finesse. He drew the two remaining trumps, crossed to dummy with ♣A, and ran ♢J. When my partner won with ♢K and was able to return yet another spade, I was able to cash two more spade tricks and collect an 800 penalty.

When ♡Q held the first round of trumps, West should have turned his attention to diamonds, leaving ♡6 in dummy as a counter to any more spade forces by the defence. The best North can do is to win ♢K, cash ♡A and return another spade, but West has retained control; he can draw the remaining trumps and collect four diamond tricks to go just one down. −200 on the East-West cards would have given them a very good match-point score, for 4♠ was unbeatable for North-South.

(11) *Always bear in mind that playing in a suit contract offers you an extra tactical manoeuvre—the ruffing finesse.*

The ruffing finesse operates when the declarer has a sequence of honours in one hand and a ruffing possibility opposite, and it attempts to trap an honour held by one of the opponents. Opportunity for this type of play occurs surprisingly often, but it is not always immediately recognised. For example, I know to my cost that my partner overlooked the extra chance offered by the right ruffing finesse on the following interesting hand from rubber bridge:

NORTH
♠ A Q J 9
♡ 7
♢ A Q J 10 9 8
♣ 9 8

SOUTH
♠ —
♡ Q J 8 5 2
♢ 7 6
♣ A K Q J 5 3

We had quite a reasonable auction to reach 6♣:

NORTH	SOUTH
1♢	2♣
2♠	3♡
3NT	4♣ (1)
4♢	5♣
6♣ (2)	NB

(1) In my view, my partner should have jumped to 5♣ at this point to show his solid suit.
(2) It seemed likely to me that 6♣ would depend on little more than a finesse.

West led ♡K and switched to ♢3. My partner went up with ♢A, cashed ♠A, throwing his remaining diamond, and ran ♢Q, losing to West's king. West now returned a trump, and my partner ended up two down.

This line of play was obviously incorrect, for South had no re-entry to dummy even if he succeeded in ruffing out East's ♢K. My suggested solution to declarer's problem is as follows. Win ♢A and cash ♠A, discarding your losing diamond. Ruff a spade, ruff a small heart in dummy and ruff another spade. Now lead ♡Q and ruff out West's ace. Provided the adverse hearts are 4-3 and the clubs 3-2, you are now home: you ruff another spade, draw the outstanding trumps and cash two established hearts for twelve tricks.

My suggested line of play depends on normal breaks in both hearts and clubs, and might fail if West holds ♡A-K-x-x and East holds ♣10. Nevertheless, I feel that 6♣ is a reasonable contract. Even without the help provided by West's opening lead, 6♣ still depends on nothing more than a successful diamond finesse—and a small slam on a simple finesse is just about worth bidding.

A Leading Question

Tips on the Opening Lead

A LEADING QUESTION

Some of the most difficult decisions to be made by a bridge player occur at the moment when he has to select his opening lead. There are a number of standard opening leads, of course, but his choice of lead in situations which are not straightforward will often distinguish the expert player from the rest: it seems to me that the great majority of average players look for indifferent, passive leads like the "top of nothing" or a trump—or, in some cases, the card nearest their thumb. The expert player, on the other hand, is inclined to favour attacking leads, knowing that he can often defeat a shaky contract by taking a slight risk and going into the attack right from trick one.

I personally find that I choose my opening lead according to a number of standard principles, as follows:

(1) *Avoid trump leads as often as possible.*

Trump leads do the declarer's work for him and often give him a trick or a tempo—or both. I can recall two dramatic occasions on which an opening trump lead proved to be absolutely fatal. The first occurred during the European Championships in Athens. I was doing the Vu-Graph commentary on the Great Britain versus Germany match, and I watched the British pair reach a very dubious slam with the following holding in trumps:

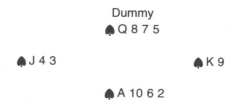

Dummy
♠ Q 8 7 5

♠ J 4 3   ♠ K 9

♠ A 10 6 2

Left to his own devices, South might well have played ♠ A and small to the queen and lost two trump tricks. After the opening lead of ♠ 3 from West, however, declarer captured East's king with the ace and fired back ♠ 10 to pick up the entire suit without loss.

My second example occurred during the Ladies Trials many years ago. One optimistic pair reached 7♠ when the full trump suit was distributed as follows:

Dummy
♠ K 9 8 7

♠ J 6 4   ♠ Q 2

♠ A 10 5 3

One down, of course. That is, until West kicked off with ♠ 4 and the defenders' trump trick vanished into thin air.

(2) *Against no trumps, don't lead your fourth highest if you want partner to switch to another suit.*

While I am not a proponent of the modern idea of "attitude" leads against no trumps, whereby a small card indicates a good suit and a not-so-small card a not-so-good suit, I certainly do not think that you should always stick rigidly to the fourth highest lead.

For example, imagine that you, West, hold the following hand:

♠ K Q 9 5 3
♡ A 8 7 6
◇ J 7 6
♣ J

and that the opponents have bid as follows:

NORTH	EAST	SOUTH	WEST
1♣	NB	1♠	NB
2♣	NB	3♣	NB
3♡	NB	3NT	NB
NB	NB		

What would you lead?

It is clear that the opponents have a good fit in clubs. Your spades are not quite good enough to make it worthwhile attacking in declarer's first suit, and the fact that your partner was unable to bid 1◇ over North's 1♣ opening makes it unlikely that his diamond suit will be good enough to defeat the contract. By a process of elimination, therefore, you should arrive at a heart lead. Furthermore, since you know from your hand that a spade switch by your partner could well prove to be the correct defence, my view is that you should not lead ♡6, the normal fourth highest lead: lead ♡8, suggesting to your partner that you do not necessarily want him to continue to plug away in the heart suit.

This was the full deal:

```
              ♠ A
              ♡ K J 9 5
              ◇ 10 2
              ♣ A 10 8 7 6 2

♠ K Q 9 5 3        N           ♠ 7 4 2
♡ A 8 7 6      W       E       ♡ Q 10 2
◇ J 7 6            S           ◇ Q 9 4 3
♣ J                           ♣ K 5 4

              ♠ J 10 8 6
              ♡ 4 3
              ◇ A K 8 5
              ♣ Q 9 3
```

At the table, West made the well-judged lead of ♡8 and declarer inserted ♡9 from dummy. East won with ♡10 and immediately switched to a small spade to ensure the defeat of the contract. As you will see, declarer could only make his contract by going boldly up with ♡K on the first trick; he can then drive out ♣K and come to one spade, one heart, two diamonds and five clubs before the defenders are able to develop their fifth trick.

A LEADING QUESTION

(3) *If partner passes your take-out double, a trump lead from you should be automatic.*

Although average players often pass a take-out double because they are unable to think of anything better to do, this is quite wrong. Such a pass should be based on a long and fairly solid holding in the opener's suit and, rather than allow the declarer to make some cheap ruffing tricks, the defenders should normally be planning to draw the declarer's small trumps and leave the way clear for the take-out doubler to cash his tricks in the three side suits.

Here is a recent hand on which the defenders successfully applied the principle outlined above. East dealt at love all.

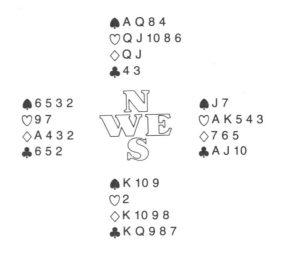

The hand layout:

North
♠ A Q 8 4
♡ Q J 10 8 6
♢ Q J
♣ 4 3

West
♠ 6 5 3 2
♡ 9 7
♢ A 4 3 2
♣ 6 5 2

East
♠ J 7
♡ A K 5 4 3
♢ 7 6 5
♣ A J 10

South
♠ K 10 9
♡ 2
♢ K 10 9 8
♣ K Q 9 8 7

The bidding was soon over:

EAST	SOUTH	WEST	NORTH
1♡	Double (1)	NB	NB (2)
NB			

(1) I don't believe in passing on this kind of hand; the good distribution makes up for the slight shortage of points, and unless partner makes a forcing response, you can always show the nature of your holding by passing on the next round. Once you have decided to bid at all on the hand, a double is clearly preferable to a simple overcall of 2♣, for it invites partner to compete in any one of three suits.

(2) A perfect hand for converting a take-out double into a penalty one: North has good values and a sufficiently robust heart holding to suggest that the defenders might well be able to draw trumps.

South led ♡2 against 1♡ doubled, and the unfortunate East went three down to concede −500. The excellent trump lead restricted East to the four tricks which he had when he started: two top hearts and two side-suit aces.

(4) Unless you have a very good reason not to, always lead your longest suit against a no trump contract.

This was a favourite slogan of the late British champion, Leslie Dodds, and I must say that I am in complete agreement; I am certain that, unless partner has bid a suit during the auction, it will work out best in the long run if you always lead your own long suit.

I was reminded of this principle by a hand from a recent teams event.

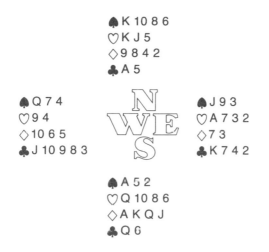

```
                    ♠ K 10 8 6
                    ♡ K J 5
                    ◇ 9 8 4 2
                    ♣ A 5
    ♠ Q 7 4            N            ♠ J 9 3
    ♡ 9 4         W       E         ♡ A 7 3 2
    ◇ 10 6 5          S             ◇ 7 3
    ♣ J 10 9 8 3                    ♣ K 7 4 2
                    ♠ A 5 2
                    ♡ Q 10 8 6
                    ◇ A K Q J
                    ♣ Q 6
```

The bidding:

SOUTH	WEST	NORTH	EAST
1◇	NB	1♠	NB
2NT	NB	3NT	NB
NB	NB		

As you will see, the natural lead of ♣J would have established four club tricks to go with ♡A for the defence, and would have given the declarer absolutely no chance. In practice, however, my partner led ♡9, and South had no difficulty in making eleven tricks.

I did not like my partner's choice of lead at the time, and I have not changed my mind since. He knew from his own hand that I must have fair values, and yet I had not overcalled in hearts; it was therefore most unlikely that my heart suit would be good enough to defeat the contract, and West had no good reason not to make his normal long-suit lead in clubs. There are, of course, exceptions to this principle, as there are to all general principles in bridge, but it would be very difficult to teach anybody all the exceptions: the only comprehensive way of learning them is by experience.

A LEADING QUESTION

(5) *It will generally pay to lead a high card from a suit headed by the king-queen.*

Most tables of standard leads suggest that, at no trumps, you should lead your fourth highest card from holdings like K-Q-x-x and K-Q-x-x-x. I do not agree. It is so humiliating to lead a low card in these circumstances and present declarer with a trick with the singleton jack or J-x that I always kick off with the king from such holdings. The worst that can happen is that you will block the suit if partner has J-x or A-x, or save the declarer a nasty guess if the situation is something like:

J 7 2

K Q 8 5 3   10 6

A 9 4

However, I regard this as a small price to pay for the certainty that you will never hand the declarer a cheap trick on a plate.

Consider the interesting hand in (Fig. I), from a team-of-four contest; North dealt at game all.

At my table, the bidding was as follows:

NORTH	EAST	SOUTH	WEST
NB (1)	1◇	NB	1NT
NB	2◇	NB	3◇
NB	3♠	NB	4♠
NB	5◇	Double (2)	NB
NB	NB		

(Fig. I)

    ♠ J 7
    ♡ K Q 9 8 3
    ◇ 9 3
    ♣ A 10 9 5

♠ 6 4 2   ♠ A Q 9 5
♡ A J 4   ♡ 10
◇ Q 7 6 4   ◇ A K J 8 5 2
♣ J 8 4   ♣ 3 2

    ♠ K 10 8 3
    ♡ 7 6 5 2
    ◇ 10
    ♣ K Q 7 6

(1) I personally would have opened this hand with 1♡. As I mentioned in Chapter 3, I always like to open, even on relatively weak hands, when I have a good suit and an obvious rebid. You will hardly ever get into trouble by opening 1♡ on this hand, for you have an easy rebid over any response from your partner; furthermore, you have indicated a good opening lead to your partner if the opponents eventually play the hand.

(2) I doubled 5◇ because of my good holding in spades and because I thought that my partner may have a trump trick or two. I was completely wrong on this second point, but we still managed to collect +500 from 5◇ doubled.

I comforted the opponents by pointing out that 4♡ was cold on the North-South hands and that their team-mates would probably reach it if North elected to open the bidding as dealer. In actual fact, it was East-West who reached game at the other table. My team-mates came to rest in the fragile contract of 3NT, and West made nine tricks when North led a low heart from K-Q-9-8-3, conceding the inevitable trick. My team therefore collected +500 in one room and +600 in the other.

(6) *Always look for an attacking lead against a small slam contract.*

As we shall see when we analyse the best of the Bols Bridge Tips in a later chapter, the great Italian champion Benito Garozzo is a firm believer in attacking against small slam contracts. I am sure he is right. Just occasionally you will be in the happy position of being able to cash two immediate tricks against the opponents' six contract. In the vast majority of cases, however, you will have just one obvious trick coming your way, and you may well have to take immediate steps to establish a second trick which you can cash at the same time. It is therefore imperative to derive the maximum advantage from your right to make the opening lead, and you must use the opportunity to search for one of the two tricks which your side has to make in order to defeat the contract.

Before selecting your opening lead against a small slam, you must try to interpret the opponents' bidding and build up a general picture of the distribution of their two hands. This is the only way in which you will be able to decide where best to direct your attack at trick one.

As a good illustration of this principle, consider the deal in Fig. II, which occurred recently at London's newest bridge circle, the St. James's Bridge Club. Irving Rose, who runs the Club so efficiently, was South; West dealt at game all.

(II)

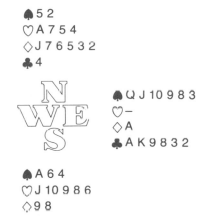

The bidding was as follows:

WEST	NORTH	EAST	SOUTH
1NT (1)	NB	3♠	NB
3NT	NB	4♣	NB
4♠	NB	5NT (2)	NB
6♠	NB	NB	NB

(1) 15–17 points.
(2) The Grand Slam Force, asking partner to bid seven with two of the top three honours.

Irving Rose paused to consider his opening lead. The fact that East was only interested in the quality of his partner's trump support implied that he held all the remaining controls and a basically two-suited hand. Rose therefore reasoned that the obvious heart lead would be ineffective, and he hit upon a more attacking lead: if East's club suit was really long, there was a possibility that North might hold a singleton in the suit. If North also held at least two spades, a plausible defence existed and Rose played for that slight chance: he led a small club, won the first round of spades with the ace and gave his partner a second-round club ruff to defeat the contract.

This hand confirms one of my favourite theories: most contracts can be defeated if you try hard enough.

A LEADING QUESTION

(7) *Always lead your partner's suit unless you have a compelling reason not to.*

In my view, there are three very good reasons for leading partner's suit on almost every occasion. In the first place, it is likely that the suit which he has bid is the one in which he has the best holding; to lead his suit will therefore develop high-card tricks for the defence. Secondly, if the opponents are playing in a no trump contract, it is almost always best to try to develop the long suit which is held by the player who has bid: he is probably the one with the side-suit entries necessary to establish and cash his long suit. Finally, and perhaps most significantly, leading his suit will keep your partner happy. If you faithfully lead his suit and fail to find an inspired alternative, partner will be very understanding; if, on the other hand, you look elsewhere for your opening lead and come up with an unfortunate and unsuccessful choice, partnership morale will be very seriously affected.

Here is a hand from the 1978 World Pairs Olympiad in New Orleans on which an expert player decided not to lead his partner's suit—with fatal results.

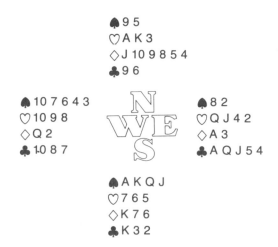

♠9 5
♡A K 3
◇J 10 9 8 5 4
♣9 6

♠10 7 6 4 3   ♠8 2
♡10 9 8   ♡Q J 4 2
◇Q 2   ◇A 3
♣10 8 7   ♣A Q J 5 4

♠A K Q J
♡7 6 5
◇K 7 6
♣K 3 2

This was the bidding when the eventual winners of the Pairs Championship, Brazilian stars Gabino Cintra and Marcelo Branco, held the North-South cards.

EAST	SOUTH	WEST	NORTH
1♣	1NT	NB	3NT
NB	NB	NB	

If West had made his natural lead of ♣7, Branco would have had no play for his contract. However, West made a mistake which is often made by players of average standard: he assumed that, just because the opponents had bid no trumps over his partner's 1♣ bid, they must have a rock-solid holding in the suit. He therefore selected ♠4 as his opening salvo, and Branco was back in with a chance. He had to bring in dummy's diamond suit with the loss of only one trick, and he knew that East had most of the missing high-card strength. He won the spade lead, crossed to dummy with ♡A and led ◇J. When East played low, Branco realised that he would have to play East for A-x or A-x-x; if East had A-Q-x in diamonds, he would win the second diamond with the ace and lead back a heart to sever declarer's communications with dummy.

Branco therefore went up with ◇K and, when both honours tumbled on the second round of diamonds, he had eleven tricks for a huge match-point score.

The Case for the Defence

Tips on Defensive Play

THE CASE FOR THE DEFENCE

In my opinion, defence is the most difficult aspect of bridge, and certainly the most difficult aspect to teach. Good defence often requires careful thought, accurate counting, vivid imagination and good rapport with your partner. I would not claim to be able to teach all those skills in one small book, let alone in one small chapter of one small book, but my hope is that the following Tips will help to show you the way in which you should be thinking if you are keen to improve your defensive play.

Most contracts can be made. However, most contracts can also be defeated, and the defenders must seize upon the slightest slip by the declarer.

As far as I am concerned, to produce a good defence is one of the most satisfying parts of the game. You can therefore imagine how pleased I was at the end of the following hand from a recent pairs tournament, even though my partner and I were only struggling to defeat a modest 2NT contract.

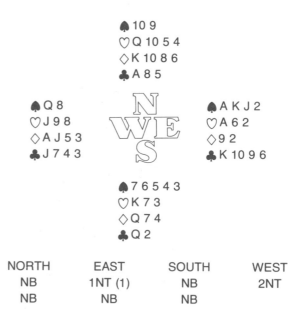

NORTH	EAST	SOUTH	WEST
NB	1NT (1)	NB	2NT
NB	NB	NB	

(1) 15–17 points.

I led ♠4 against 2NT. Dummy's ♠Q held the first trick, and my partner played ♠10, which I assumed was from 10–9 doubleton. Declarer led a small club to ♣10 at trick two, and I was in with ♣Q. I realised that I had to find my partner with a good holding in hearts if we were to have any chance of defeating 2NT, and I therefore switched to ♡3. East played ♡8 from dummy and allowed my partner's ♡10 to hold the trick. North returned ♡4, declarer ducked again, and I won with ♡K and paused to take stock.

The play so far had marked East with ♠A-K-J, ♡A and presumably one top honour in clubs. He was therefore most unlikely to hold ◇K as well and, since we were clearly not going to take enough tricks in hearts to defeat the contract, I tried the effect of ◇4 at the fifth trick. This proved to be the killing defence. North won with ◇10 and returned a diamond to my ◇Q, and we now had six defensive tricks: two hearts, two diamonds and two clubs.

As you will probably have already noticed, East could have made his contract by winning the first or second round of hearts and driving out ♣A. However, my experience is that declarers often make minor technical errors of this kind, and it is up to the defenders to take full advantage of the slightest slip.

Always bear the bidding in mind when you are planning your defence—you will pick up vital clues about the two unseen hands.

One of my Tips on Dummy Play in Chapter 5 was that the declarer should always bear the opponents' bidding in mind while he is playing the hand. The same point applies to a defender when he is striving to defeat the contract: in his case, however, he must cast his mind back to any bidding done by both the declarer and the other defender.

West overlooked this vital point on the following hand, dealt by him at game all.

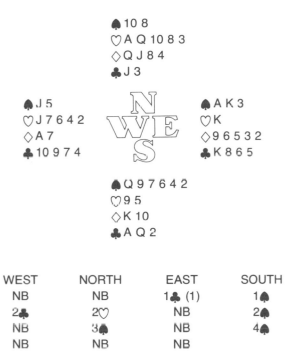

```
                    ♠ 10 8
                    ♡ A Q 10 8 3
                    ◇ Q J 8 4
                    ♣ J 3

  ♠ J 5                            ♠ A K 3
  ♡ J 7 6 4 2        N             ♡ K
  ◇ A 7           W     E          ◇ 9 6 5 3 2
  ♣ 10 9 7 4         S             ♣ K 8 6 5

                    ♠ Q 9 7 6 4 2
                    ♡ 9 5
                    ◇ K 10
                    ♣ A Q 2
```

WEST	NORTH	EAST	SOUTH
NB	NB	1♣ (1)	1♠
2♣	2♡	NB	2♠
NB	3♠	NB	4♠
NB	NB	NB	

(1) It is unusual to open a four-card suit in preference to a five card suit, but East realised that his side was unlikely to play the hand and he certainly did not want his partner to lead a diamond.

West led ♣10 against 4♠, and East covered dummy's ♣J with the king. South won with ♣A, ruffed a club in dummy and led a diamond to ◇K in an attempt to establish a discard for his losing heart. West won with ◇A and switched to a heart, but South had already decided that ♡K must be in the East hand to justify his opening bid. He therefore went up with ♡A, dropping East's singleton king, and landed his ambitious contract by playing East for precisely A-K-x of trumps: he led ♠10 from dummy, which East won with ♠A, and subsequently crossed to hand with ◇10 to lead ♠Q, pinning West's jack.

South read the hand well and it was obvious that he had listened carefully to the bidding. Unfortunately, the same could not be said of West. At the point when he gained the lead with ◇A, he knew that his partner had 6 points at the most in hearts, diamonds and clubs. East was therefore marked with top spade honours, and West should have fired back a second diamond instead of switching to a heart. East could then return a third round of diamonds after winning the first spade with the ace, and West's ♠J would become the setting trick.

THE CASE FOR THE DEFENCE

When you are defending, try to count where your tricks are going to come from to defeat the contract—and then play accordingly.

There is nothing more annoying for a defending side than to develop enough tricks to defeat the contract, and then find themselves unable to cash them. In many cases, such ignominy can be avoided if the defenders count their tricks carefully and then plan ahead. East and West did just that on the following hand, dealt by South at love all.

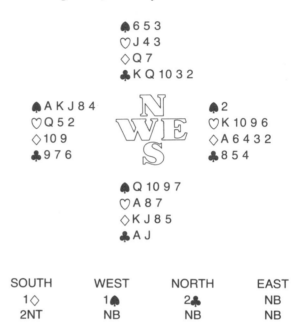

♠ 6 5 3
♡ J 4 3
◇ Q 7
♣ K Q 10 3 2

♠ A K J 8 4
♡ Q 5 2
◇ 10 9
♣ 9 7 6

♠ 2
♡ K 10 9 6
◇ A 6 4 3 2
♣ 8 5 4

♠ Q 10 9 7
♡ A 8 7
◇ K J 8 5
♣ A J

SOUTH	WEST	NORTH	EAST
1◇	1♠	2♣	NB
2NT	NB	NB	NB

West led ♠K and was depressed to see his partner's discouraging ♠2. Realising that the defenders would have to look to the heart suit for their tricks, West found the excellent switch of ♡2 at trick two. East won with ♡9 and returned ♡6, which South ducked again, and West was in with ♡Q. He now made another excellent defensive play by cashing ♠A before returning his third heart. South could only cash seven tricks without establishing a diamond, and East was able to win ◇A and cash his fourth heart to defeat the contract.

West's reasoning is instructive. The fact that East returned a heart rather than a spade at trick three confirmed West's fears that declarer held four spades. The sequence of play in the heart suit made it clear that East must hold ♡K-10-9-x, and East had to hold a quick trick in one of the minor suits if the defence was to have any chance of defeating the contract. If this assumption was correct, the defenders could take three hearts, either a club or a diamond, and two spades—but only if West cashed his second top spade while he still could.

This hand occurred in a large international pairs event, and very few defenders managed to collect six tricks against a no trump contract. In fact, several declarers made nine tricks after an initial small spade lead from West.

Don't put all your eggs in one basket when you are defending. If you are not certain how the contract is to be defeated, plan your defence in such a way that you keep all your options open.

This Tip is once again very similar to one which I gave on declarer's play in Chapter 5. My advice there was: "Don't put all your eggs in one basket. Where you have more than one hope of making your contract, you must make certain that your sequence of play combines all available chances." Exactly similar principles apply when you are defending, as the following example shows:

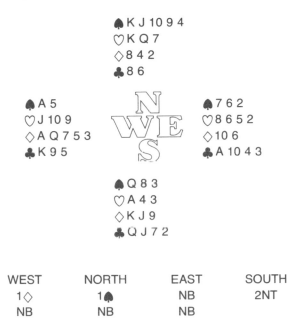

♠ K J 10 9 4
♡ K Q 7
◇ 8 4 2
♣ 8 6

♠ A 5
♡ J 10 9
◇ A Q 7 5 3
♣ K 9 5

♠ 7 6 2
♡ 8 6 5 2
◇ 10 6
♣ A 10 4 3

♠ Q 8 3
♡ A 4 3
◇ K J 9
♣ Q J 7 2

WEST	NORTH	EAST	SOUTH
1◇	1♠	NB	2NT
NB	NB	NB	

West leads ◇5, and South captures ◇10 with ◇J. Declarer immediately plays on spades and West takes ♠A on the second round, noting that his partner signals an odd number of cards in the suit.

The play to the first trick marked South with ◇K-J-9, and, in order to defeat the contract, West has to find his partner with a second diamond and either ♡A or ♣A. The natural switch might appear to be ♡J, but this can be shown to be quite wrong. West should switch to ♣5. If the worst comes to the worst and declarer has ♣A-Q, the club switch will give him two club tricks—but only seven tricks in all. East will still have time to win the first round of hearts with ♡A and return the vital diamond. If, on the other hand, West switches to ♡J and it is South who holds ♡A, there will never be an opportunity to play a club: declarer will have four spades, three hearts and one diamond—and his contract.

THE CASE FOR THE DEFENCE

Following similar principles enabled me to find the correct solution for defeating a contract during an important pairs event. This was the full deal:

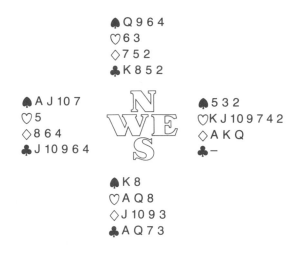

```
                    ♠ Q 9 6 4
                    ♡ 6 3
                    ◇ 7 5 2
                    ♣ K 8 5 2

♠ A J 10 7              N              ♠ 5 3 2
♡ 5                 W     E           ♡ K J 10 9 7 4 2
◇ 8 6 4                S              ◇ A K Q
♣ J 10 9 6 4                          ♣ –

                    ♠ K 8
                    ♡ A Q 8
                    ◇ J 10 9 3
                    ♣ A Q 7 3
```

The bidding was identical at several tables:

EAST	SOUTH	WEST	NORTH
4♡	Double	NB	NB
NB			

When I held the South hand, I led ◇J against 4♡ doubled. Declarer won with ◇K, my partner contributing ◇2, and immediately played ♡K. I won with ♡A and was confronted with a problem which was faced by several defenders hòlding the South cards.

A number of defenders reasoned that in view of his pre-emptive opening bid, East was most unlikely to hold ♣K as well as ♡K-J and ◇A-K-Q. They therefore switched to a club at trick three, and declarer was home. He knocked out ♡Q, drew trumps and took two finesses in spades to land ten tricks in some comfort.

I reasoned that there was no hurry to switch to a club, for declarer would not be able to discard any losing clubs on dummy's spades while I still held two trumps. I therefore switched to ♠K at trick three, and that proved to be the killer blow. If East captured ♠K with dummy's ♠A, I could collect a spade ruff by returning a second spade after winning with ♡Q; and if East ducked ♠K, she would ultimately lose two spades and two hearts to suffer a one-trick defeat.

Even if you have found an unlucky opening lead, it may pay you to persevere with that suit rather than take a chance elsewhere.

Although most textbooks offer the reader a wide selection of spectacular and flamboyant defensive plays and coups, this is probably not a true reflection of bridge at the actual table. My experience is that one of the secrets of good defence is to know when to remain passive and when to spring into dynamic action. Furthermore, my experience is that a relatively passive defence will be a perfectly adequate counter to at least half of the opponents' contracts, and I like nothing more as declarer than to play against defenders who switch frantically from suit to suit.

It is always tempting to search for a sparkling switch when you have selected a perfectly reasonable opening lead which has worked out poorly for your side. Quite often, however, it will pay you to resist this temptation and to persevere with your original suit. This is the kind of deal which I have in mind.

South opened 1NT and everyone passed. West had no particularly attractive opening lead, and his actual selection of ♠2 worked out poorly when South guessed correctly and played low from dummy. East played ♠Q, and South won with ♠K and led ♣J. West won with ♣A, and paused to assess the situation.

West realised that his opening spade lead had conceded a trick. However, there was no obvious switch to be made, and West decided not to make things worse by opening up another suit. He therefore exited passively with a second spade and South, left to his own devices, ended up with only six tricks. He won the spade return with ♠J and played a club to ♣10 and another club. East cashed two clubs and pushed back another spade, and South was now compelled to open up the diamond suit. This enabled the defenders to make three clubs, three diamonds and one hard-earned spade trick.

As you will see, West found the only defence to give his side a chance of defeating the contract. If he had won ♣A and switched to a heart or a diamond, or returned a second club, South would have had a comfortable ride to seven tricks.

THE CASE FOR THE DEFENCE

It will generally help your partner if you signal to show your length in a suit which the declarer is playing, but make sure that you don't help the declarer more by giving him useful information.

I generally find that it helps the defence if both defenders signal their distribution in the suits played by the declarer. To peter, or play high-low, shows an even number of cards in the suit, and to play your small cards from the bottom upwards shows an odd number. To give a count in this manner can be helpful in many ways, but the principal advantages are (a) that it assists the defenders to obtain a clearer idea of the declarer's length in other more crucial suits, and (b) that it makes it easier for the defenders to count the declarer's likely tricks.

The hand seen in Fig. I is a good advertisement for distributional signals.

(Fig. I)

```
              ♠ A 7 4
              ♡ A K 9 2
              ◇ 8 6 5
              ♣ 9 5 4

♠ K J 9 5 3      N        ♠ 10 2
♡ J 6         W     E     ♡ 10 7 5 4 3
◇ Q 4           S        ◇ 9 3 2
♣ A J 7 2                 ♣ K 6 3

              ♠ Q 8 6
              ♡ Q 8
              ◇ A K J 10 7
              ♣ Q 10 8
```

SOUTH	WEST	NORTH	EAST
1◇	1♠	Double (1)	NB
1NT	NB	2NT	NB
3NT	NB	NB	NB

(1) A so-called "Sputnik" double. In the modern style, this suggests a four-card heart suit and asks the opener to describe his hand further.

West led ♠5, and East's ♠10 lost to declarer's ♠Q. South cashed ◇A, on which East contributed ◇2, and crossed to dummy by playing ♡Q and a small heart to ♡A. He now finessed ◇J, losing to West's ◇Q, and West paused to consider the evidence of the play so far.

The fact that East had played his small diamonds in ascending order meant that both he and declarer had begun life with an odd number of cards in the suit. This placed South with a five-card diamond suit, and West could count nine tricks which were now available for declarer: two spades, three hearts and four diamonds. He therefore had to play for the only remaining chance of defeating the contract—that East held K-x-x or K-x-x-x in clubs. A small club switch by West after he gained the lead with ◇Q produced the four tricks which were urgently required for the defence.

Let us now suppose that South's hand in the above diagram were slightly different, say:

```
              ♠ Q 8 6
              ♡ Q 8
              ◇ A K J 10
              ♣ K 8 6 3
```

A club switch by West would now be absolutely fatal, establishing South's ♣K as his ninth trick. However, West would no longer have any reason to switch to a club, provided that his partner faithfully signalled his suit lengths. In this case, East would play ◇3 followed by ◇2 to show an even number of cards in the suit, presumably four; he would also play ♡3 followed by ♡4 to show an odd number of cards in hearts, presumably five. This invaluable information will enable West to calculate that declarer can only have eight readily available tricks: two spades, three hearts and three diamonds. He will therefore fire back ♠K after winning with ◇Q, and the contract should be defeated by one trick.

I must give one word of warning about distributional signals. If you are contemplating showing your length in a suit which is being played by the declarer, make sure that the information is likely to help your partner rather than the declarer. For example:

♣ Q 10 4 2

♣ J 9 5 3   ♣ 8 7

♣ A K 6

If both East and West peter when the declarer cashes the ace and king of clubs, West must not feel too aggrieved if South finesses dummy's ♣10 on the third round.

It is perfectly possible to give a suit preference signal at the first trick—but only if there is no other meaning to be attached to the signal.

One of the most common old wives' tales in bridge is that you cannot play suit preference signals at trick one. I have never understood this. If you have no other message to convey to your partner at the first trick, concerning either high cards or distribution, there is no reason why you should not indicate your preference between the other suits.

A neat example of such a signal occurred during the Teams Championship at the Geneva O.R.T. Charity Tournament in 1978 (Fig. II). East dealt at game all.

(II)

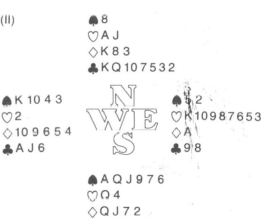

EAST	SOUTH	WEST	NORTH
Schoen		Mrs. Markus	
4♡	4♠	Double	NB (1)
NB	NB		

(1) North, who after all held the best hand at the table, must have been slightly surprised by all the goings-on.

I led ♡2 and declarer went up with dummy's ace. It was quite obvious from the bidding that my partner held ♡K, and in any case he knew that my ♡2 was a singleton. He therefore took the opportunity to indicate a preference for diamonds by playing ♡10 at the first trick, and this made the subsequent defence much easier.

After winning ♡A, declarer immediately finessed ♠Q, losing to my king. I cashed ♣A and, in response to my partner's earlier suit preference signal, switched to a diamond. East won with ◇A and returned a small heart for me to ruff. A diamond ruff and a third round of hearts now promoted my ♠10 into a fourth trump trick, and this made the penalty +800.

The excellent result we achieved on the above deal helped my scratch British team on its way to a surprise victory in the Geneva teams event. We were complete outsiders in a strong international field, and I still get a tremendous thrill from a victory of this kind. The thrill of winning is, in fact, one of the principal reasons why I still enjoy playing the game so much. I am also intrigued by the fact that no matter how much I play, I continue to come across new situations and have new decisions to take. Finally, I enjoy travelling to so many lovely places to play in bridge festivals and to collect interesting material for my books and articles. I used to play a lot of rubber bridge, and the excitement of playing for high stakes gave me a great deal of pleasure—probably because I was usually showing a profit when I left the table. Nowadays, however, my writing work and my bridge travels take up so much of my time that I am not able to play as much rubber bridge as I would like.

Here is another example of a suit preference signal at trick one paving the way to a good result. South dealt with East-West vulnerable.

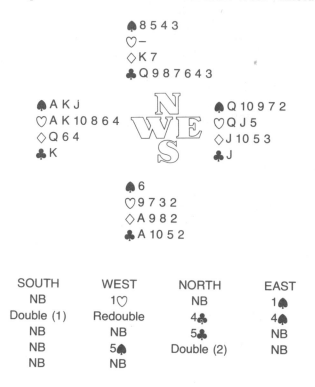

	♠ 8 5 4 3	
	♡ –	
	◇ K 7	
	♣ Q 9 8 7 6 4 3	

♠ A K J		♠ Q 10 9 7 2
♡ A K 10 8 6 4		♡ Q J 5
◇ Q 6 4		◇ J 10 5 3
♣ K		♣ J

	♠ 6	
	♡ 9 7 3 2	
	◇ A 9 8 2	
	♣ A 10 5 2	

SOUTH	WEST	NORTH	EAST
NB	1♡	NB	1♠
Double (1)	Redouble	4♣	4♠
NB	NB	5♣	NB
NB	5♠	Double (2)	NB
NB	NB		

(1) Showing the two unbid suits and reasonable defensive values. With a hand with greater length in the minor suits and less high-card strength, South would bid 1NT or even 2NT over 1♠.

(2) The inference that his partner held worthwhile defensive values enabled North to make a well-judged double of 5♠.

South led ♣A, and the first trick consisted of ♣A, ♣K, ♣Q and ♣J. North's spectacular play of the queen could only be a suit preference signal, and South obliged by switching to a heart at trick two. A heart ruff, ◇K, ◇A and a second heart ruff set the contract by three tricks, and North-South's excellent defence had netted them +800. As it happened, they needed to collect a substantial penalty from 5♠ doubled, for their two hands fitted so well that 5♣ was unbeatable and even six can be made because of the favourable distribution.

The Bols Bridge Tips

BOLS BRIDGE TIPS

I would like to explain to my readers why I have included the Bols Bridge Tips in this book.

The Bols Tips are probably not too easy to follow and understand for the average player, but they contain most valuable information and have great instructional value. All it needs for the average reader is some concentration and effort to follow the thinking of the expert. It is not so long ago that ordinary players looked vague when the "Stayman convention" was mentioned. Today it is a very popular method and one can hardly understand how we could have lived without it for so long.

I tried to be fair to all those experts who produced their special Bols Bridge Tips. Some of them probably tried to be too original, others too complicated. I personally do not like them all, but I thought it would be fair to present them to my readers and to let them make their choice. I would advise you to try them out, to give them a chance and to adopt only those which give you pleasure and seem to you useful on the right occasion.

I have repeatedly stated that I am not in favour of playing too many complicated methods, which does not mean that we should not try all the time to improve our game and learn to follow the expert when he shows us the right way. Take your pick and if some of the Tips seem to you difficult to understand, then just ignore them, but I am sure that all of you will find some valuable instruction if you are looking for it.

The Bols Bridge Tips Competition obviously owed its existence primarily to the Bols Liquor Company of Holland. However, they were sold the idea by Herman Filarski, the Dutch author and bridge expert, and our own Albert Dormer did a great deal to promote the contest.

The competition took the following form. Over the three years 1975 to 1977, twenty-four top-ranking experts were invited to submit a Bridge Tip which would help ordinary players in awkward situations that arise fairly frequently. The entries each year were judged by a jury of nearly forty members from several different countries and, although some of us did not always agree with the results, the jury's decision was always accepted with good grace.

Omar Sharif, after a bridge session.

The Bols Bridge Tips Competition was won in 1975, the first year of the contest, by England's Terence Reese. His advice to the declarer was to follow the early discards and ask himself: From what holding would the defender most readily have made those discards? The answer will often resolve a critical guess.

Reese wrote as follows:

"A defender who holds A–5–3–2 or K–5–3–2 will discard from that suit more readily than if he had held Q–5–3–2 or J–5–3–2. This will give you a clue in situations of this kind:

(I)	J 7 6		(II)	J 8 6 2	
Q 9 4		A 5 3 2	A 5 3		Q 9 4
	K 10 8			K 10 7	

This is a side suit in a trump contract and declarer needs to establish one fast trick. In (I) East has made two early discards. Conclusion: he is more likely to hold A–x–x–x than Q–x–x–x. In (II) West makes an early discard. Conclusion: he is more likely to have discarded from A–x–x than from Q–x–x.

(III)	A 8		(IV)	K 10 8	
J 9 4		K 7 5 3 2	A 5 3 2		J 7 6
	Q 10 6			Q 9 4	

In (III) East makes two early discards. When you play the ace and 8 he follows with the 5 and 7. Play him for K-x-x-x-x rather than J-x-x-x-x. In (IV) West discards twice. He is more likely to have come down to A-x than to J-x; but if a low card to the king is headed by the ace, be inclined to play East for A-J-x.

"Such inferences are especially strong when dummy has what may seem to a defender to be an establishable suit, as in Fig. I.

"South plays in 4♠ after the following sequences:

SOUTH	NORTH
1♠	1NT
3♠	4♠
NB	

"West leads ♣3 and South ruffs the third round. There is something to be said for leading a heart at once, putting West under some pressure if he holds the ace. However, the declarer plays four rounds of trumps, discarding a diamond from dummy. West throws a club and a diamond, East a club and a heart.

"After cashing three diamonds, South leads a heart and West plays ♡8. South should finesse ♡J. Why? Because of East's heart discard. With A-9-x-x, East, expecting the contract to depend on the heart guess, would not think it necessary to keep all four. But with Q-9-x-x, he would not let go a heart, in case declarer held A-x.

"As so often, the discard tells the story."

(Fig. I) Dealer South; love all.

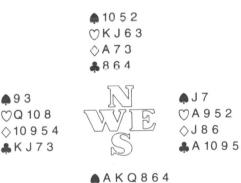

```
              ♠ 10 5 2
              ♡ K J 6 3
              ♢ A 7 3
              ♣ 8 6 4
♠ 9 3                         ♠ J 7
♡ Q 10 8        N            ♡ A 9 5 2
♢ 10 9 5 4    W   E          ♢ J 8 6
♣ K J 7 3       S            ♣ A 10 9 5
              ♠ A K Q 8 6 4
              ♡ 7 4
              ♢ K Q 2
              ♣ Q 2
```

I have often come across hands on which, as Terence Reese suggests, an apparently harmless early discard by a defender should give the declarer a vital clue to the winning line of play. One which springs to mind occurred in the Great Britain versus France match in the European Ladies' Championship in Elsinore in 1977:

```
                    ♠ K Q 9 4 2
                    ♡ A 9 5 3
                    ◇ 2
                    ♣ 6 5 3
   ♠ 10 8 6                            ♠ —
   ♡ 10            N                   ♡ Q J 7 4 2
   ◇ K J 7 6 5 4  W   E               ◇ 10 9 8
   ♣ K 9 2          S                 ♣ Q 10 8 7 4
                    ♠ A J 7 5 3
                    ♡ K 8 6
                    ◇ A Q 3
                    ♣ A J
```

Both North-South pairs reached the poor contract of 6♠. When Miss Michelle Brunner was the declarer for Britain, West made the helpful lead of ♡10. This enabled South to win in dummy with the ace and subsequently lead towards ♡K-8 to develop a third heart trick with dummy's ♡9 for a crucial club discard.

At the other table, Miss Nicola Gardener made the better opening lead of a small trump from the West hand, although she also failed to find the killing club attack. Declarer drew trumps and had the problem of how to develop a third heart trick for a club discard. If the adverse hearts were 3-3, of course, there would be no problem, and her task would also be simple if either defender held the doubleton Q-J, Q-10 or J-10.

In fact, there was another slight chance which became a distinct possibility at the table. On the third round of trumps, East discarded a small heart. As East could see four hearts in dummy, this was most unlikely to be from a four-card holding. Similarly, she would be unlikely to discard from a three-card heart holding when she would have ten minor suit cards from which to choose. The early heart discard was therefore quite likely to be from five, and in this case there would be a 50-50 chance of West's singleton heart being an honour. The correct play was therefore to cash ♡A first, with the intention of establishing a third heart trick by force if a singleton honour appeared from West.

Tip No. 2, the tip placed second in the first Bols Competition, was submitted by Brazilian star Gabriel Chagas. It introduced a new aspect to the finesse.

"The finesse is usually regarded as one of the humbler forms of play, but it sometimes requires quite a lot of imagination. This is especially true of the intra-finesse.

Q 8 5 3

J 7   K 10 4

A 9 6 2

"The bidding has given you a good idea of the layout of this suit. To hold yourself to one loser, you play small towards the queen and finesse the 8. East will score the 10, but later you'll enter the North hand and lead the queen, smothering West's jack. This is an intra-finesse.

"Now try the play in 4♡ on the next deal; West has overcalled in clubs.

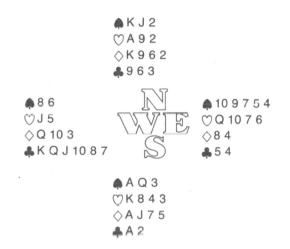

♠ K J 2
♡ A 9 2
◇ K 9 6 2
♣ 9 6 3

♠ 8 6   ♠ 10 9 7 5 4
♡ J 5   ♡ Q 10 7 6
◇ Q 10 3   ◇ 8 4
♣ K Q J 10 8 7   ♣ 5 4

♠ A Q 3
♡ K 8 4 3
◇ A J 7 5
♣ A 2

"You duck the first club and West continues the suit. As a 3-3 trump break is unlikely, you lead a low heart towards the dummy and, when West follows with ♡5, you finesse ♡9.

"East wins with ♡10 and switches to a spade, confirming that the clubs are 6-2. You cash the ace of trumps and, when this collects the jack from West, you pick up East's remaining trump by finessing ♡8.

"On the fourth trump you throw not a club but a diamond from dummy. The successful intra-finesse has brought you to nine tricks, but now you must establish a diamond for game. As you are wide open in clubs, you lead a low diamond, intending to finesse ◇9 into East's hand. West, however, inserts ◇10. You win with dummy's king and cash the remaining spades. When West shows out on the third spade, you have a perfect count. West began with six clubs, two hearts and two spades—and therefore three diamonds.

"You need no more finesses. On the third spade, West is forced down to two diamonds and ♣J. You therefore lead dummy's losing club, throwing West in and forcing him to lead into your diamond tenace.

"My Bols Bridge Tip, therefore, is that whenever you have to develop a shaky suit, and especially when this suit is trumps, you should consider whether you can prepare for an intra-finesse by ducking with an 8 or a 9 on the first round."

BOLS BRIDGE TIPS

3. The Seres Tip

Third place in the 1975 Bols Competition went to Tim Seres, who left war-torn Hungary as a youth and went to live in Australia. By the middle of the 1950s, he had become the outstanding bridge player in his new country, and he has remained their Number One player ever since. Tim's tip was entitled "Give Declarer Enough Rope":

"In the long haul, you win at bridge by avoiding error rather than by being brilliant. The expert may display an occasional glimpse of genius or elegance, but he owes his pre-eminence to the fact that he makes fewer mistakes than his fellow players.

"Because bridge is a game of errors, you should try to develop the knack of giving an opponent the chance to go wrong. One way of doing this is by providing the declarer with a choice of plays in a situation where he would otherwise be bound to make a winning play.

"Opportunities for such plays come along much more frequently than many players realise. The following hand occurred in a top-class pairs event:

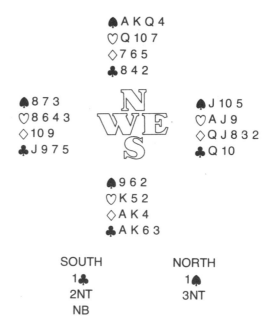

	SOUTH		NORTH
	1♣		1♠
	2NT		3NT
	NB		

"The popular contract was 3NT and West normally led ◇10, hoping to hit his partner's suit. All declarers but one succeeded easily, making four spade tricks, two diamonds, two clubs and a heart. How could a top declarer fail?

"At this table, South won the diamond lead and tested spades. On the ace and king of this suit, East dropped the jack and 10! Not surprisingly, declarer assumed that the spades were 4–2, and he continued by playing low to ♠9, hoping to re-enter dummy with a heart. But East ducked the king of hearts when it was led. The contract could now have been made only on double dummy lines, and in actual play South finished one down.

"The hapless declarer had fallen victim to a defender who followed the very profitable adage: 'Give declarer enough rope. . . .' My Bols Bridge Tip is therefore this: When you can see that declarer is bound to succeed by normal play, look for a chance to give him a losing option. It stands to reason that if you consistently give your opponent a chance to go wrong, he will sometimes take it!"

Another Tip submitted in the first Bols Competition was Tip No. 4 by Italy's Giorgio Belladonna, who is arguably the world's most successful bridge player ever. His advice was that whenever you, as a defender, include the ace of trumps among your assets, you should consider whether to hold up this card when trumps are first played. To withhold the vital ace will often leave the defenders in control of the hand.

Tip No. 5, by Charles Goren, was also on the theme of ducking. He suggested that if you aren't sure how to continue after you win a trick, you should consider ducking it. But there are many cases when you will not have time for consideration after the opportunity arises, for example when you hold the ace over K-Q-x or K-Q-10. In these situations, the duck will only be effective if you execute it smoothly, leaving declarer in doubt as to where the high card is.

Tip No. 6 was by Bobby Wolff, a member of the famous Dallas Aces team. His Tip was based on a very neat hand.

"Some of the clues concerning the unseen hands are rather obvious: an opponent who opened the bidding is likely to have at least thirteen points, and so on and so forth.

"Obvious—but not always entirely reliable. The successful declarer does not rest content with these easy clues but tries to unearth additional information. This challenging hand from match play shows the process at work (Fig. II). East dealt at game all.

(II) North: ♠9875 ♡AJ83 ◇KQ7 ♣82. West: ♠— ♡10962 ◇AJ100054 ♣54. East: ♠KJ42 ♡KQ74 ◇2 ♣A963. South: ♠AQ1063 ♡5 ◇93 ♣KQJ107.

EAST	SOUTH	WEST	NORTH
1♣	1♠	2◇	4♠
NB	NB	NB	

"The spade game was reached at both tables in a team-of-four game, and the play to each trick was identical. However, one declarer based his play on flimsy reasoning while the other had a sure bet.

"West led ♣5, and East took the ace and switched to ◇2. West won with the ace and returned a diamond, ruffed by East who exited with a club. This trick was won by declarer as West followed suit.

"The defenders had taken three tricks and South had to pick up the spade suit without loss. Both declarers crossed to dummy's ♡A and ran ♠9. This held the trick, and now another spade lead took care of the trumps, allowing the game to be scored.

"The first declarer remarked: 'I played for the double finesse in spades because East had opened. West had shown up with five points and I reckoned that East needed both spade honours for his bid.'

"A good reason. But is it good enough? Suppose that East had not had ♠J. Might he not have opened the bidding just the same? The singleton diamond surely would have persuaded him, so declarer did not really have valid grounds for the deep finesse.

"Why did the second declarer play West for a void in spades? The answer is hidden in both the bidding and the play. East, who had opened with 1♣, had shown up with only four cards in the suit. He therefore could not have five cards in either hearts or spades, and as he had a singleton diamond he must be precisely 4-4-1-4, so West had to be void of spades.

BOLS BRIDGE TIPS

"My Bols Bridge Tip is that you should not be content simply to work out the high cards a defender is likely to have for the bids he has made. You should try to picture his distribution, for this may provide you with an even surer guide to the winning play."

7. The Hamman Tip

Tip No. 7 was by another of the Dallas Aces, Robert Hamman, and it concerned placing the cards. Hamman suggested that if you are ever to amount to anything at bridge, you must be able to build up a picture of the unseen hands; the idea is that you must know what the problem is before you try to solve it.

8. The Markus Tip

The eighth entry in the first Bols competition was by me. Unfortunately, however, I slightly misunderstood the conditions of the competition, and I was under the impression that the theme of the Tip had to be something entirely new. I therefore chose an aspect of the play of the cards in defence which has scarcely been considered before, as follows:

"When you, as a defender, are about to attack a suit in which you have a holding such as J-x, Q-x or K-x, do you invariably lead the high card? Most players always do, but this is sometimes quite a costly mistake.

"My Bols Bridge Tip is that when you have to open up such a holding, you should consider the possible advantage of leading the low card. This may well work better when the hand on your left is marked with strength in this suit, and especially when you have no re-entry to your hand."

In actual fact, a hand with this theme had occurred when I was playing with Benito Garozzo a few years earlier. I was East on the following deal, and South played in 4♠ after I had opened the bidding with a pre-emptive 3♡ (Fig. III).

Garozzo led ♡Q against 4♠. I overtook with ♡K and declarer won the trick with ♡A. He then crossed to dummy with a club and finessed a spade to West's ♠Q. West returned a second heart to my ♡9, and I had to find the key switch. As I could see that the clubs were breaking kindly for the declarer, it seemed to me that I had to set up a diamond trick quickly and remove dummy's entry. As you will see, if I made the normal return of ◇J, West would not be able to continue the suit when he gained the lead with ♠A. I therefore found the key switch of ◇4, and this defeated the 4♠ contract, which had been made at every other table of a large pairs event.

(III)

```
                    ♠ J 4
                    ♡ 7 5
                    ◇ K 8 6 3
                    ♣ A K 9 6 2
    ♠ A Q 7                        ♠ 8 2
    ♡ Q 8 3         N              ♡ K J 10 9 6 2
    ◇ Q 9 5 2    W     E           ◇ J 4
    ♣ 8 5 3         S              ♣ Q J 10
                    ♠ K 10 9 6 5 3
                    ♡ A 4
                    ◇ A 10 7
                    ♣ 7 4
```

9. The Besse Tip

The 1976 Bols Tips event was a victory for Switzerland's leading player, Jean Besse. Besse is one of the great European card players of the post-war era, and his inventiveness has only been equalled among his contemporaries by such giants of the game as Karl Schneider, Terence Reese and Jan Wohlin. His winning Tip was entitled "Beware of your Trump Tricks":

"Bobby Fischer once said: 'You have found a very good move. Fine! This is the time to think again: there probably exists a better one.'

"Bobby, of course, was talking about chess. His advice, however, also applies to bridge—and especially to the situation where a defender sees an opportunity to make an easy trump trick. Surprisingly often, it will pay him to look for better things.

"Players soon learn that by not overruffing the queen with K-10-2 behind declarer's A-Q-J-9-8-7 they can ensure two tricks. The following, however, is less obvious (Fig. IV).

"The contract is 4♠. South ruffs the opening club lead and sets out to establish his side suit: he takes two top hearts and ruffs a heart in dummy with the queen of spades. If East yields to the temptation of overruffing with the king, South loses only one other trump trick to the ace and makes his contract.

"However, if East refuses to overruff, the declarer is bound to lose three trump tricks no matter how hard he tries. With a diamond loser in addition, he is defeated.

"The idea of not overruffing soon becomes familiar whenever you hold either length or strength in the trump suit. Somewhat less well known are those cases where the defender with the shorter or weaker trump holding may gain a trick for his side by employing the same tactics, (see Fig. V).

"The contract is 4♠, East having overcalled in hearts. West leads ♡10 and East plays off the three top cards in the suit. If, on the third round of hearts, West jumps in with ♠Q, declarer will discard from dummy and thereafter will have no trouble picking up East's trumps. Instead, West should rise to the occasion by discarding a diamond! After ruffing this trick in dummy, South will have to lose two trump tricks—and his contract.

"My Bols Bridge Tip is this: Beware of your trump tricks. When you see a chance for an easy overruff, don't be in too much of a hurry to take it. You may gain still more tricks by holding back."

(IV)
```
           ♠ Q 2
           ♡ 8 6
           ◇ K J 9 5
           ♣ Q 10 9 7 6
♠ A 9                    ♠ K 8 3
♡ Q 3 2                  ♡ 9 7
◇ Q 4 3 2               ◇ A 10 7 6
♣ A K 5 4               ♣ J 8 3 2
           ♠ J 10 7 6 5 4
           ♡ A K J 10 5 4
           ◇ 8
           ♣ —
```

(V)
```
           ♠ 9 2
           ♡ 6 5
           ◇ A K Q 4 3
           ♣ A K 5 4
♠ Q 7                    ♠ K 6 5
♡ 10 7                   ♡ A K Q 9 8 2
◇ 10 9 8 7 2            ◇ J 5
♣ J 9 6 2               ♣ 10 8
           ♠ A J 10 8 4 3
           ♡ J 4 3
           ◇ 6
           ♣ Q 7 3
```

10. The Schenken Tip

Second place in the 1976 Bols competition went to Howard Schenken, a player who has been at the centre of the contract bridge world right from the birth of the game. His record in major US championships is unapproached, and he has also made the record number of eight World Championship appearances. Schenken's Tip concerned defence at trick one.

"Much has been written about the careful thought required of declarer before he plays to the first trick. But little has been said about the player on the declarer's right—East in the normal diagram. When you are in this position, you often have a difficult but vital role to play. Unlike declarer, you cannot see your partner's hand, but by reviewing the bidding and observing the opening lead you may be able to visualise it.

"While South is thinking over his plan of attack, you may have a chance to plan your defence. Even if South plays quickly to the first trick, you should not allow yourself to be hurried. For example, see Fig. VI.

"South opens 1NT (16–18 points), North raises to 3NT and West leads ♡2. Declarer quickly plays dummy's ♡10, and of course you cover with ♡Q automatically. Or do you? Not unless you have been lulled into following suit without thinking!

"So I will assume you are concentrating and are ready to begin the chore of counting points. You and dummy each have ten, South has at least sixteen, so your partner has at most four. His fourth-highest lead shows a four-card suit with (a) no honours, (b) the king or (c) the ace.

"If partner has (a) you lose a trick by covering; with (b) you break

(VI)
```
           North
           ♠ 9 5
           ♡ J 10 4
           ◇ K Q 2
           ♣ A 10 7 5 3

                    East
                    ♠ J 10 7 2
                    ♡ Q 8 5 3
                    ◇ A 9 4
                    ♣ K 6
```

even. So you focus your attention on (c), which gives declarer K-x. In this case, of course, you must duck, and when sooner or later you come in with ♣K, your heart return defeats the contract.

"My Bols Tip is this: when you are defending in third position, cultivate the habit of playing slowly to the first trick. Careful thought will help you to defeat many more contracts."

11. The Forquet Tip

Pietro Forquet, the Italian star whose partnership with Benito Garozzo is thought by many to have been the greatest the world has ever known, took third place in the second Bols Competition. His Tip has a two-part theme: "Count the opponents' hands—but when you have counted them, play intelligently!"

"How many times have you heard the excuse: 'Sorry partner, if I'd guessed correctly I'd have made the contract.'? And how many times was this so-called 'unlucky guess' truly unlucky?

"For example, take a look at a hand that my partner played in a recent pairs event:

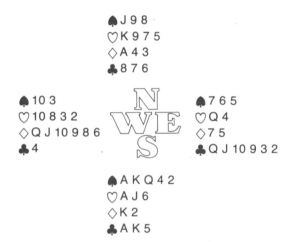

"We reached the good contract of 6♠, and my partner received the lead of West's singleton club. East played ♣9, forcing declarer's ace, and declarer continued with three rounds of trumps, ending in his own hand. Crossing to dummy with ◇A, he took the successful heart finesse. Next he cashed ♡A, dropping East's queen.

"My partner had now, as they say, reached the crossroads. The contract was guaranteed (he could count on five trump tricks, three hearts and four top cards in the minor suits), but the overtrick hinged on 'guessing' the heart position. Had East started life with the doubleton queen? Or did he have Q-10-4 initially, in which case the false card of the queen would have been mandatory on the second round? As this was a pairs event the overtrick was obviously vital, and my partner spent a good deal of time pondering his choice. In the end he played a heart to the king, hoping to drop the 10, and made only twelve tricks.

" 'Sorry, partner', he said, and explained that if he had taken the finesse for the 10—and it had failed—he would have gone down in 6♠, having no further entry in dummy. At this point I gave him my Bols Bridge Tip: count the opponents' hands!

"He should have won the third round of trumps in dummy, and then taken the heart finesse. With twelve tricks in the bag, he could now set about obtaining the vital count by playing out three rounds of diamonds, ruffing the third round. The ♣K comes next, the play to this trick revealing West's distribution: two spades, six diamonds, one club and therefore four hearts. Declarer can now finesse dummy's ♡9 for a certain overtrick and a much better score on the board."

12. The Valenti Tip

One of my favourite Tips in that second Bols Contest was that submitted by one of Italy's leading woman players, Anna Valenti. Her theme was that it can sometimes be less dangerous to play out the hand without touching trumps than to stake everything on a favourable trump break, and it seems to me that this Tip relates to a situation which frequently arises in real life. I have often watched average players draw too many rounds of trumps and then find themselves a trick short. Anna Valenti wrote as follows:

"When your trump suit consists of four trumps opposite four, you should bear in mind that the outstanding trumps will break poorly (4-1 or 5-0) about one-third of the time. If you cannot withstand such a division, you should give serious thought to playing out the hand without touching trumps. Provided you keep your head, you will be surprised how often this plan succeeds. Quite frequently you will find yourself making contracts that, to a bystander, would have seemed certain to fail. (Fig. VII.)

"You are in 4♡ and West leads ♠Q. If you try to draw trumps and establish the diamonds, there will be a danger of losing two trump tricks and two diamonds for one down. As the risk of a damaging overruff does not seem very great, the first move should be to lead not a trump but a low diamond from dummy. The 10 loses to the king and West switches to ♣J. You win in hand and cash ♠K, discarding a club from dummy.

"A low spade from hand is ruffed in dummy and ◇Q is led. East returns his singleton trump, and West's ♡8 forces the ace. Firmly in control, you cash ♣K, ruff a diamond with ♡9 and ruff your last spade in dummy.

"Ten tricks have been played and you have won eight of them. Your last three cards are ♡K-J and a losing club. As the cards lie, you have no need to finesse ♡J—you simply lead a diamond from dummy, discard your club, and wait for West to lead back into your tenace.

"Whenever there is danger of losing too many trump tricks, you should hesitate to launch a frontal assault on this suit. This is especially so when an opponent has contested the bidding, for a favourable break in your trump suit is then less likely. (Fig. VIII.)

"You play in 4♠ after West has overcalled in clubs. West begins with ♡A and switches to ♣K. If you try to draw trumps, the contract will fail. Instead, you should see how many trump tricks can be made by indirect methods. On winning with ♣A, you ruff a club and lead ♡Q. (This is safe, for if the opponents could ruff a heart they would already have done so.) If West returns a third club, you ruff, cash the heart winner and cross to ◇A to lead dummy's last club.

"Suppose that East discards a diamond. You ruff and cash ♠K and ◇K. You have won eight tricks, the defenders two. You lead a third diamond, ruffing low in dummy. East overruffs, but then has to give dummy the last two tricks.

(VII)

	North	
	♠ A	
	♡ A 7 6 5	
	◇ Q J 9 4 2	
	♣ K 8 3	

West		East
♠ Q J 10 4		♠ 9 6 3 2
♡ Q 10 8 3		♡ 2
◇ K 5 3		◇ A 8 7
♣ J 10		♣ Q 9 6 5 4

	South	
	♠ K 8 7 5	
	♡ K J 9 4	
	◇ 10 6	
	♣ A 7 2	

(VIII)

	North	
	♠ A J 7 5	
	♡ 10 7 3	
	◇ A 4	
	♣ A 7 6 2	

West		East
♠ 6		♠ Q 10 9 8
♡ A K 8 6		♡ 9 4 2
◇ 10 8 7		◇ 9 6 5
♣ K Q 10 9 8		♣ 5 4 3

	South	
	♠ K 4 3 2	
	♡ Q J 5	
	◇ K Q J 3 2	
	♣ J	

"If East elects to ruff the fourth round of clubs, you overruff with
♠K. Now you can cash two more diamonds—again bringing yourself to
eight tricks—before continuing diamonds and endplaying East as before.

"Even when your trump suit is solid, it may still be fatal to touch this
suit too early. The next example is one of my favourite hands:

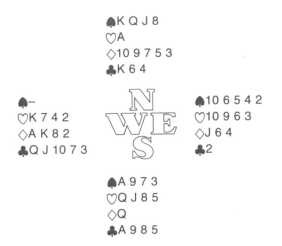

```
                    ♠K Q J 8
                    ♡A
                    ◇10 9 7 5 3
                    ♣K 6 4

    ♠-                   N             ♠10 6 5 4 2
    ♡K 7 4 2         W     E           ♡10 9 6 3
    ◇A K 8 2            S              ◇J 6 4
    ♣Q J 10 7 3                        ♣2

                    ♠A 9 7 3
                    ♡Q J 8 5
                    ◇Q
                    ♣A 9 8 5
```

"South was in 4♠ and West led ♣Q, which was taken with dummy's
king. South's first move was to lead a diamond, establishing
communications, rather than to test the trumps. West continued with
♣10, and East ruffed. East made the best return of a trump and West
showed out, dummy winning with ♠8.

"With this unfavourable development, declarer saw that she would
need a second trick in hearts. ♡A was cashed and the closed hand entered
with a diamond ruff. ♡Q was covered by the king and ruffed in dummy.
Another diamond ruff was taken, ♡J was cashed, and a heart was ruffed.
South had taken eight tricks and was able to take two more by the simple
method of crossruffing with the ace and king of trumps.

"If South had taken even one round of trumps early on, East would
have been able to play a second trump when he ruffed the club, leaving
declarer with only nine tricks.

"My Bols Bridge Tip is this. Don't rush to draw trumps. On some
hands you may be unable to draw them successfully; on others, even if
you succeed in drawing trumps, you may find that you are left with too
few tricks. On all these hands, you should consider whether it is better to
make as many tricks as you can by crossruffing."

I also liked Jeremy Flint's Tip in the second Bols competition, although that, too, was unplaced. He was concerned with the vital subject of the opening lead, and he spotlighted some common situations where the best card to lead from a three- or four-card holding headed by an honour is not necessarily the orthodox low card. This is Tip No. 13 in my summary of the Bols Tips.

"It is normal in bridge to lead low from a suit of three or more cards headed by an unsupported honour card. There are, however, some basic situations where the lead of the high card may produce better results.

"The most common of these occurs when there has been a competitive auction. Suppose that the defender on lead has, say, K-x-x-x of his partner's suit and scarcely any other assets. It may very well be good play to start with the king in order to retain the lead and find the killing switch through the dummy.

"Experienced players will recognise that kind of situation readily enough. Here is a case where a little more thought is required. The bidding has been:

SOUTH	NORTH
1♣	1♠
2◇	2♠
2NT	3NT
NB	

West has to lead from:

♠ K 10 7
♡ Q 10 4
◇ Q 3 2
♣ J 9 7 6

"The opponents' bidding suggests that they have little to spare. Furthermore, South has displayed lukewarm enthusiasm for his partner's suit. For that reason it is good play to attack with a spade. No other lead appeals, and declarer may well be embarrassed by an early assault on dummy's entry.

"Having reached that conclusion, the best card to lead is the king. Declarer may misjudge the lie of the suit—or the king may even score a trick by force. In play this was the full deal (Fig. IX):

"Not unnaturally declarer allowed ♠K to win. On the next trick he received a nasty shock when ♠J lost to the queen. He elected to discard a heart. Now, after a heart switch and continuation, he was limited to six tricks.

"At the other table, after a heart opening lead, South succeeded in scrambling home with two heart tricks, four clubs, two diamond tricks and a spade.

"My Bols Bridge Tip, therefore, is that instead of stolidly pushing out an unimaginative small card from three or four to an honour, you should consider whether to lead the honour."

Strangely enough, Jeremy Flint's Bols Tip was the exact opposite of mine: whereas I was recommending leading the low card in situations where you would normally lead an honour, he was suggesting leading the honour in situations where you would normally lead a low card.

(IX)

```
                  ♠ A J 9 8 4 3
                  ♡ J 3 2
                  ◇ J 7
                  ♣ 10 2
   ♠ K 10 7              N        ♠ Q 6 5
   ♡ Q 10 4          W       E    ♡ K 7 6 5
   ◇ Q 3 2              S        ◇ K 8 6 4
   ♣ J 9 7 6                      ♣ 5 3
                  ♠ 2
                  ♡ A 9 8
                  ◇ A 10 9 5
                  ♣ A K Q 8 4
```

BOLS BRIDGE TIPS

The following hand from a recent international pairs tournament is a good illustration of Jeremy Flint's Tip in operation in actual play:

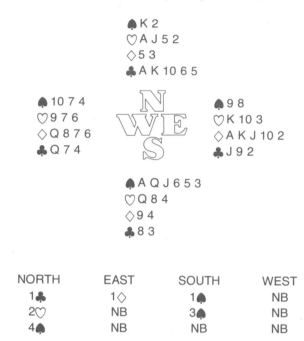

```
              ♠ K 2
              ♡ A J 5 2
              ◇ 5 3
              ♣ A K 10 6 5

  ♠ 10 7 4          N           ♠ 9 8
  ♡ 9 7 6       W       E       ♡ K 10 3
  ◇ Q 8 7 6         S           ◇ A K J 10 2
  ♣ Q 7 4                       ♣ J 9 2

              ♠ A Q J 6 5 3
              ♡ Q 8 4
              ◇ 9 4
              ♣ 8 3
```

NORTH	EAST	SOUTH	WEST
1♣	1◇	1♠	NB
2♡	NB	3♠	NB
4♠	NB	NB	NB

When I was the declarer in 4♠, West led ◇Q and his partner contributed ◇J. West now got the message and switched to a heart at trick 2, and I was held to ten tricks and +420. This was a very poor match-point score for us. At other tables, West led the more orthodox ◇6 to ◇3, ◇K and ◇9, and East did not dare to underlead ◇A at the second trick. ♡A therefore remained in dummy as an entry to the established clubs and most declarers escaped for the loss of two diamond tricks, scoring the vital overtrick which can be so important in a pairs event.

Juan les Pins, dramatic encounter between John Collings – Terrence Reese and Omar Sharif – Leon Yallouse.

Tip No. 14 was by US star James Jacoby, one of the original Dallas Aces. His theme was that it pays to be highly suspicious. Whenever an opponent does something which is seemingly helpful to your side, you should look for the ulterior motive. In fact, beware of bridge players bearing gifts!

Pierre Jais' Bols Tip concerned the vital subject of defensive signalling, and he suggested that you can effect quite an improvement in your defensive play by enlarging the use of suit-length signals to cover additional situations.

"Practically everybody knows how to use suit-length signals on the first round of a suit: you play high-low to show an even number of cards, low-high to show an odd number. In this diagram you are East and your partner leads ♡K.

♡J 8 4

♡K Q 9 7   ♡6 5 3 2

♡A 10

"On the lead of the king you start an echo with ♡6, showing an even number. So far, so good—but what happens when the cards are divided like this?:

♡J 3 2

♡K 9 5 4   ♡Q 8 7 6

♡A 10

"This time West leads ♡4, dummy plays low and your queen loses to the ace. Later, your partner gains the lead in another suit and lays down ♡K. In certain circumstances it could be vital for West to know that South started with only two hearts. In fact, if there is no outside entry to dummy, West will be able to switch to another suit and declarer may never come to a second heart trick.

"My suggestion is that, as East, you should echo—or not echo—with your remaining cards in order to show how many you still have. In the above example, where East has three cards left in hearts, he should follow suit with ♡6 on the second round. With Q-7-6 originally, East would follow with ♡7 on the second round, starting an echo to show two cards remaining."

BOLS BRIDGE TIPS

16. The Rubens Tip

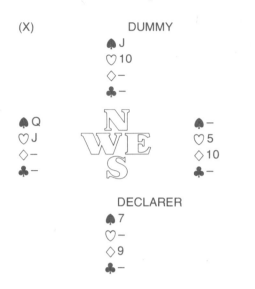

(X)　　　　　　DUMMY

　　　　　　♠ J
　　　　　　♡ 10
　　　　　　◇ –
　　　　　　♣ –

♠ Q　　　　　　　　♠ –
♡ J　　　　　　　　♡ 5
◇ –　　　　　　　　◇ 10
♣ –　　　　　　　　♣ –

　　　　　　DECLARER

　　　　　　♠ 7
　　　　　　♡ –
　　　　　　◇ 9
　　　　　　♣ –

From left to right, Strumpher Dr. Loeben-Sels, Rixi Markus, President of World Bridge Federation – Jimmy Ortiz, Patino Evelhnsenn, Hermann Filarski (Dutch journalist and champion) Albert Dormer (author and player) Derek Rimington (computer expert but most efficient as a player and bridge writer) enjoying the generous hospitality at the Bols factory.

The third Bols Bridge Tip Competition was held in 1977 and it was won by Jeff Rubens, the co-editor of the excellent American *Bridge World* magazine. His Tip, which is my favourite Bols Tip of them all, was on the subject of partnership co-operation, and he stressed that a defender should be aware of his partner's problems as well as his own. The Rubens Tip, which is No. 16 in my summary, is entitled "Honour Thy Partner".

"Car A signals for a left turn but then starts to turn right and suddenly brakes to a stop. Whereupon Car B, travelling behind A at a normal distance and speed, crashes into a tree.

"Bridge 'crashes' are often of this sort. One of the defenders makes a losing play but his partner was at fault. There is not only a loss on the deal, but also a drop in partnership morale. We seem to mind more when partner causes us to make the fatal move than when he makes it himself.

"A player should be alert to partner's problems as well as his own. Everyone tries to help his partner by signalling, but better players should aim to go further still.

"For example, a good partner tries to remove undesirable options. If you fear that partner may duck his ace in front of dummy's king-jack, you can prevent this by leading the suit yourself. If you cannot get in to lead the suit, perhaps you can discard the queen behind dummy's king-jack!

"One measure of a defender's thoughtfulness is how he plays in the sort of situation seen in Fig. X.

"East is on lead at no trumps and does not know who has ♡J. But he does know that West has ♠Q. Leading ♡5 cannot lose a trick no matter who has ♠7 and ♡J. Leading ◇10 also cannot lose a trick—*provided West guesses correctly which card to keep*. A strong defender will not let his partner face this guess.

"Where players often fall down is in failing to notice that partner may have a problem. Once the problem is seen, protective measures are usually quite simple (see Fig. XI).

SOUTH	WEST	NORTH	EAST
1♣	NB	1♠	NB
1NT	NB	3NT	NB
NB	NB		

"West leads ♡7 to 9, ace and 2. As East, what do you return?

"In play, East mechanically returned his remaining heart and it was natural for West (who needed only for East to have another heart and one entry) to duck. The defence was now separated from its five tricks and declarer made his contract.

"West played the fatal card—but ♡K was 'lost' by East. His immediate heart return could accomplish nothing except giving West a headache. East should lead something else at trick two—♣8, for example. When East leads his remaining heart later, West knows that he is not expected to duck, and now the contract must fail. Note that nothing is lost in the unlikely event that West has king-jack of hearts.

"You can keep even a sleepy partner from harm by removing his losing choice altogether.

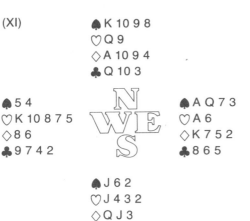

(XI)

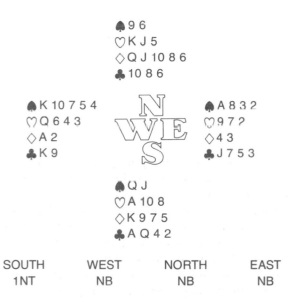

SOUTH	WEST	NORTH	EAST
1NT	NB	NB	NB

"West led ♠5 to 6, ace and jack. East returned ♠2 to queen, king and 9. As West, how do you plan the defence?

"West can see seven tricks for the defence: five spades, one diamond and one club. But unless East leads a club early in the play, South will strike first with two hearts, four diamonds and one club.

"The average West, having reasoned this far, leads ♠4 at the third trick. Then East may win and unthinkingly return a spade. West will win the argument that follows, but South will make his contract. A good defender scores points before the post-mortem by playing ♠7 before leading the 4. When East wins he is out of spades and has no alternative to the winning club switch.

"My Bols Tip is: Honour Thy Partner. Show that you treat his problems as your own and actively help him solve them. Amazingly, this will improve not only partner's defence but also his overall performance. He will be playing more carefully in order to be worthy of your respect."

BOLS BRIDGE TIPS

After winning the third Bols Tips competition, Jeff Rubens produced a number of additional examples with the same theme. He also suggested that any play which has as its sole object the provision of help for partner should be given a special name: the Bols Coup.

The following follow-up article by Jeff Rubens first appeared in the Bulletin of the International Bridge Press Association:

"One of the most common situations in which one can apply the 'Bols Coup' is when telling your partner whether, and if so how, to give you a ruff.

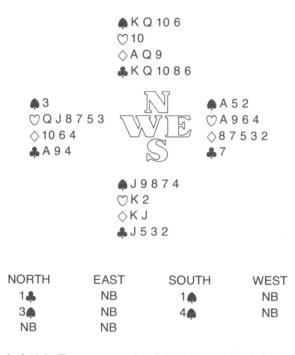

NORTH	EAST	SOUTH	WEST
1♣	NB	1♠	NB
3♠	NB	4♠	NB
NB	NB		

"West led ♡Q. East won and quickly determined that there was no hope for the defence unless West held ♣A. He therefore played his singleton club at trick two.

"West made a similar determination—he needed to assume East held ♠A. If so, South almost certainly held ◇K, considering East's passing and South's bidding. A singleton club with East seemed unlikely, so West decided to play East for a doubleton club. Hoping that South held distribution such as 5-2-3-3, West ducked his ♣A to preserve his entry opposite East's hypothetical doubleton. Thus, the defence lost its club ruff.

"As in many of these situations, West's correct play opposite an unthinking partner is debatable. But there is no question that East should have saved his problem by *cashing* ♠A before switching to clubs. This would leave West no option but to reach the winning conclusion.

"A defender looking for an immediate ruff is not always so fortunate as to be dealt the ace of trumps.

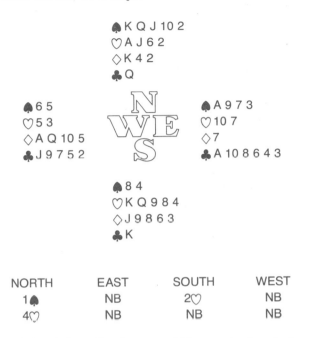

♠ K Q J 10 2
♡ A J 6 2
♢ K 4 2
♣ Q

♠ 6 5
♡ 5 3
♢ A Q 10 5
♣ J 9 7 5 2

♠ A 9 7 3
♡ 10 7
♢ 7
♣ A 10 8 6 4 3

♠ 8 4
♡ K Q 9 8 4
♢ J 9 8 6 3
♣ K

NORTH	EAST	SOUTH	WEST
1♠	NB	2♡	NB
4♡	NB	NB	NB

"West led a club to East's ace and East made the obvious switch to ♢7. South covered with the 8 and West (looking to East to hold ♠A or ♡K and at least one more diamond—hardly an unlikely set-up) made the obvious play of ♢10. South then made a few obvious plays of his own, and wound up discarding three diamonds on dummy's spades, making his contract.

"Obvious or not, West's defence was reasonable. East's was not. He should have removed his partner's losing choice by *cashing* ♠A before leading his diamond. (If South ruffs, there was no hope for the defence anyway.)

Fiesta in Portugal in the famous wine caves after a bridge session in the Algarve. Georgio Belladonna sings and dances and everyone joins in.

BOLS BRIDGE TIPS

(XII)

```
            ♠ A 10 9 5
            ♡ A Q
            ◇ 4 3 2
            ♣ K Q 10 7

♠ 2                          ♠ K 7 3
♡ 8 7 5 3      N             ♡ J 10 9 6 4 2
◇ 9 8 7 5    W   E           ◇ A Q 10
♣ A 6 5 2      S             ♣ 8

            ♠ Q J 8 6 4
            ♡ K
            ◇ K J 6
            ♣ J 9 4 3
```

"Even when you cannot informatively cash a winner, it may be possible to prevent partner from suffering from the results of his own calculations (Fig. XII).

NORTH	EAST	SOUTH	WEST
1NT	NB	3♠	NB
4♠	NB	NB	NB

"West led ◇9. East, upon winning the ace, thought he recognised a routine position and switched to ♣8. Matters turned out to be somewhat less than routine when West, after some thought, ducked. Another ruff lost; another contract that slipped away.

"East had no immediate way of giving West the needed clue, but he did have a method available. All East had to do was *do nothing*. If East had simply returned a diamond, declarer would have won, played hearts if necessary, and attacked spades. East, upon winning his ♠K, would lead his club and West (with any holding he could have from East's point of view) would be able to work out that a club return couldn't hurt.

"Not all ruff-signals take place in the timing of the ruffer's plays.

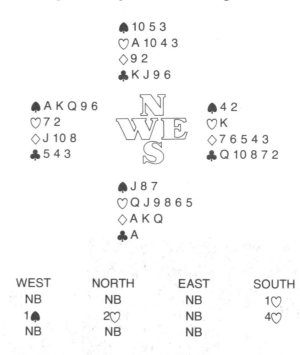

```
            ♠ 10 5 3
            ♡ A 10 4 3
            ◇ 9 2
            ♣ K J 9 6

♠ A K Q 9 6                  ♠ 4 2
♡ 7 2          N             ♡ K
◇ J 10 8     W   E           ◇ 7 6 5 4 3
♣ 5 4 3        S             ♣ Q 10 8 7 2

            ♠ J 8 7
            ♡ Q J 9 8 6 5
            ◇ A K Q
            ♣ A
```

WEST	NORTH	EAST	SOUTH
NB	NB	NB	1♡
1♠	2♡	NB	4♡
NB	NB	NB	

"West started with ♠A K Q. East lackadaisically threw a diamond and West, thinking South might have something like ♠J-8-7 ♡K-Q-J-9-8 ◇A-K ♣A-7-2, exited 'safely' with a diamond. South won and led ♡Q, but he did not finesse. West had passed originally with ♠A-K-Q-x-x, so declarer went up with dummy's ♡A as his only chance. South was lucky and the defenders discovered they had something to talk about—a fourth round of spades from West would have sunk the contract.

"West could not have known this. East had known it, and he should have transmitted the information by *discarding* ♣Q on the third spade. This ostensibly nonsensical play, implying lack of interest in taking a club trick, would direct West's attention to the necessary trump promotion.

"As in most realms of defensive play, some signals are more subtle than others. As a group, the signals that tell partner *not* to try for a ruff are more difficult to produce than those encouraging a ruff.

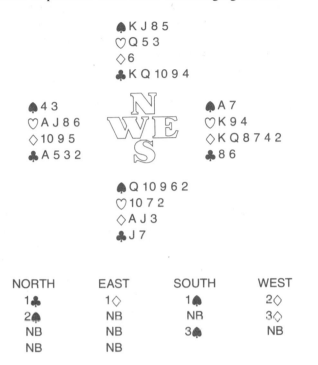

```
                    ♠ K J 8 5
                    ♡ Q 5 3
                    ◇ 6
                    ♣ K Q 10 9 4
    ♠ 4 3                              ♠ A 7
    ♡ A J 8 6          N               ♡ K 9 4
    ◇ 10 9 5      W        E           ◇ K Q 8 7 4 2
    ♣ A 5 3 2         S               ♣ 8 6
                    ♠ Q 10 9 6 2
                    ♡ 10 7 2
                    ◇ A J 3
                    ♣ J 7
```

NORTH	EAST	SOUTH	WEST
1♣	1◇	1♠	2◇
2♠	NB	NB	3◇
NB	NB	3♠	NB
NB	NB		

"West led ◇10 to the 6, queen and ace. South led ♠10 to East's ace and East, appreciating the value of having West lead hearts first, switched to ♣8.

"West saw his duty clearly. He won ♣A and returned ♣5 for his partner to ruff. He hoped to get in with ♡A and give his partner another ruff to defeat the contract. But South won the second club lead, drew trumps and took eleven tricks. East pointed out the result of a ♡J switch by West instead of the second club. In fact, however, East had a clear chance to solve West's problem, although few players would think of the correct play. He should have held up the ace of trumps for one round before leading clubs. It is not only that this play would put West off the idea of getting two ruffs, but also that in ambiguous situations holding off with a trump trick (if not required for other purposes) suggests lack of interest in getting a ruff. Had East done this, West would have been warned against trying for a club ruff— and his best play is to switch to ♡J."

17. The Truscott Tip

Dorothy Truscott, the American star who is one of only two women who have played in a contest for the Bermuda Bowl, the blue riband of international team bridge, finished second in the 1977 Bols Contest with a Tip on defensive signalling. In actual fact, her suggested methods have been in fairly common use in this country for a number of years under the name of Smith Peters, after I. G. Smith of Winchester.

"Suppose West leads ♠4 against 3NT, and sees this:

DUMMY
9 7

WEST   EAST
A 10 8 4 2   J

DECLARER
K

"Dummy plays ♠7, East plays the jack and declarer wins with the king. Who has the queen? West can't tell. If he gets the lead in some other suit, should he try to cash his spades or should he wait for partner to lead the suit?

"My Bols Tip is this: Against no trumps, a defender's first small card, unless it is essential to give a count, should indicate attitude towards the opening leader's suit.

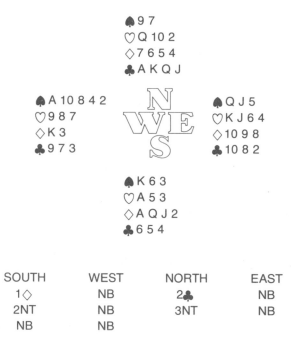

♠9 7
♡Q 10 2
◇7 6 5 4
♣A K Q J

♠A 10 8 4 2   ♠Q J 5
♡9 8 7   ♡K J 6 4
◇K 3   ◇10 9 8
♣9 7 3   ♣10 8 2

♠K 6 3
♡A 5 3
◇A Q J 2
♣6 5 4

SOUTH	WEST	NORTH	EAST
1◇	NB	2♣	NB
2NT	NB	3NT	NB
NB	NB		

"West leads ♠4 against 3NT and declarer wins East's jack with the king. Declarer leads a club to dummy. East should play ♣10 on this trick, meaning: 'I love your lead, partner. Please continue.' Declarer takes a diamond finesse and when West wins the king he cashes four spade tricks for down one.

"Now suppose that the East and South cards had been slightly different, as in Fig. XIII:

"The bidding, the opening lead and the play to the first trick are the same as before. Again declarer leads a club to dummy, but this time East can't stand a spade continuation from partner so he contributes ♣2.

"Declarer takes a diamond finesse, losing to the king. West now knows he can't afford to continue spades from his side of the table, and he exits with ♡9. East grabs the trick, returns ♠6, and the contract fails by two tricks.

"Note that in both these cases West would have been on a complete guess without the 'attitude' signal. And if he had guessed wrong twice, declarer would have made both games."

(XIII)

```
              ♠ 9 7
              ♡ Q 10 2
              ◇ 7 6 5 4
              ♣ A K Q J
♠ A 10 8 4 2            ♠ J 6 5
♡ 9 8 7                ♡ A J 6 4
◇ K 3                  ◇ 10 9 8
♣ 9 7 3                ♣ 10 8 2
              ♠ K Q 3
              ♡ K 5 3
              ◇ A Q J 2
              ♣ 6 5 4
```

18. The Priday Tip

Third place in the 1977 Competition went to our own Tony Priday, whose Tip was on the always fascinating subject of deceptive play in defence.

"Military men give much thought to camouflage. Thus a general, when planning a defensive battle, will pretend to be strong in a part of the line where he is weak. He will also try to appear vulnerable in a place where he is strong.

"Defenders at bridge have many opportunities to do the same. When you are strong in a suit, you aim to conceal the fact. There is then a good chance that declarer will misread your strength in another—and perhaps vital—suit. Equally effective is to pretend to hold more strength than you actually possess, and this deal shows how you can easily recognise that type of situation when it occurs, as in Fig. XIV.

SOUTH	WEST	NORTH	EAST
1♡	NB	1NT	NB
2♠	NB	2NT	NB
4♡	NB	NB	NB

"You may not approve of North's bidding, but that is the way the auction went in the final stages of Britain's Gold Cup some years ago.

"West led ◇A and, when his partner encouraged with ◇7, continued with ◇3. East took the second trick with the jack and realised that South's shape was almost certainly 5-6-2-0. In that case, declarer might well have to take a vital guess in spades. East therefore set out to camouflage his spade holding.

"At the third trick, East laid down ♣K! Declarer ruffed with a high trump and entered dummy with a heart to lead ♠10. Convinced that East must hold ♣A, declarer placed West with ♠A and so ran ♠10. West therefore won with ♠Q, and East's ace provided the setting trick in due course.

"My Bols Tip is this. When you are defending, remember the art of camouflage. If you can mislead declarer in one suit, he may well jump to a wrong conclusion in another suit."

(XIV) Dealer South; game all.

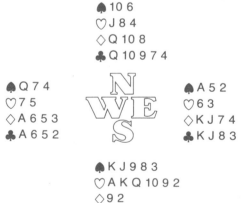

```
              ♠ 10 6
              ♡ J 8 4
              ◇ Q 10 8
              ♣ Q 10 9 7 4
♠ Q 7 4                ♠ A 5 2
♡ 7 5                  ♡ 6 3
◇ A 6 5 3              ◇ K J 7 4
♣ A 6 5 2              ♣ K J 8 3
              ♠ K J 9 8 3
              ♡ A K Q 10 9 2
              ◇ 9 2
              ♣ —
```

It was just as well that my opponent had not read Tony Priday's Tip before the following hand from an international pairs tournament two or three years ago. East dealt with North-South vulnerable.

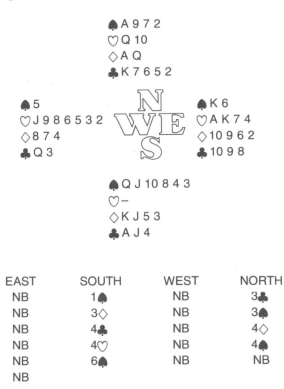

EAST	SOUTH	WEST	NORTH
NB	1♠	NB	3♣
NB	3◇	NB	3♠
NB	4♣	NB	4◇
NB	4♡	NB	4♠
NB	6♠	NB	NB
NB			

West led ♡6 against my contract of 6♠, and I ruffed East's ♡K and immediately ran ♠Q. East won with ♠K and exited with his remaining spade, and the fate of my slam contract depended on my handling of the club suit. In normal circumstances, I would have taken a second-round finesse of ♣J and bemoaned my luck when both black-suit finesses were wrong. On this occasion, however, I had a vital clue to drop the doubleton ♣Q: the play to the first two tricks marked East with ♠K and ♡A-K, and his failure to open the bidding therefore made it most unlikely that he held ♣Q as well.

East should, of course, have camouflaged his holding of hearts by playing ♡A at trick one. I would then have had no reason to place ♣Q in the West hand and I would have gone one down by making the normal percentage play of the second-round club finesse.

Tip No. 19 in my summary was by Brazilian star Pedro-Paulo Assumpcao. His Tip was on the subject of declarer's play, and he stressed the importance of not just doing the right things but of doing them in exactly the right order.

"In most deals, declarer soon identifies the plays he must make for the contract, such as establishing a suit or knocking out an entry. But however good his reasoning, success may still elude him unless he makes these plays in precisely the right order. In bridge, the secret is often in the timing.

"On the following deal, three distinct steps are needed and there is only one correct sequence.

```
                    ♠ 10 6 5
                    ♡ K 6 4
                    ◇ 8 4 2
                    ♣ K 9 8 2

      ♠ Q 9 4           N           ♠ J 7
      ♡ J 10 8       W     E        ♡ A 9 7 3 2
      ◇ Q J 5 3         S           ◇ 10 6
      ♣ Q 10 4                      ♣ J 6 5 3

                    ♠ A K 8 3 2
                    ♡ Q 5
                    ◇ A K 9 7
                    ♣ A 7
```

SOUTH	WEST	NORTH	EAST
1♠	NB	1NT	NB
3◇	NB	3♠	NB
4♠	NB	NB	NB

"West leads ♡J and you win with the queen. You hope for a 3-2 trump break, but you may still need to look after the fourth diamond. The plan, therefore, must be to draw two rounds of trumps, give up a diamond, and ruff a diamond. The question is, what is the best timing?

"If you start with two top trumps, West will cash ♠Q when in with a diamond and dummy will not get a ruff. Suppose, then, that you begin with three rounds of diamonds. Still no good, for West will play a fourth diamond and East will overruff the dummy.

"The solution is to start by ducking a diamond. Then you simply cash A-K of trumps and go on your way rejoicing. You could easily miss this solution unless you were actively searching for the best timing, and my Bols Tip is this: When more than one play is needed to make the contract, give special thought to the best sequence. You may well find that the order in which you make your plays is no less important than the plays themselves."

BOLS BRIDGE TIPS

20. The Eisenberg Tip

Tip No. 20 was contributed by Billy Eisenberg, another member of the original Dallas Aces team. His Tip was also on the subject of declarer's play, and he suggested a number of situations in which the declarer should play low instead of high from dummy in an attempt to cause the third player to commit an unnecessarily high card. For example, it might gain a trick to duck in dummy if West leads a small card in the following situations:

(a) NORTH	(b) NORTH	(c) NORTH
K J 7 5	Q J 6	A J 3
SOUTH	SOUTH	SOUTH
–	5	7

It will not always be easy for East to make the correct play of inserting the 8 or 9, and South will obviously be better off if East panics into playing a top honour.

21. The Sundelin Tip

Swedish star Per-Olov Sundelin's Tip was intended to emphasise the axiom that if a contract cannot be defeated by normal play, the defenders should be willing to adopt abnormal measures. He wrote as follows: "Be bold when you are defending. If you can't see yourself beating the contract by winning the trick, duck it—even at the cost of a trick. By deceiving declarer, you may yet cause his house of cards to collapse."

22. The Lebel Tip

Tip No. 22 was by the young French expert Michel Lebel. He recommended a new and daring form of defensive hold-up play to destroy the declarer's communications:

"Successful defence often requires that you should take all possible measures to shut out dummy's long suit. Often you try to ruin declarer's communications. Sitting over dummy's K-Q-10-9-x, you may hold off with A-J-x when declarer plays up to dummy's king.

"It can even be good play to hold up the jack from A-J-x when declarer finesses dummy's 10 on the first round. My Bols Tip, however, is that you should sometimes hold up the jack even when you do not possess the ace.

"You will find that quite remarkable results can be obtained. When the following deal (Fig. XV) first occurred, I held the East cards:

"South opened 1NT, North raised to 3NT and West led ♡3, East's jack losing to declarer's king. South played a low diamond to dummy's 9 and East, without any hesitation, allowed ◇9 to win. South quite naturally came back to his hand with a spade and repeated the finesse. When ◇10 lost to the jack, South was very disappointed; his shortage of entries to dummy meant that he could no longer make nine tricks.

"It is easy to see that the contract cannot be defeated if East wins the first round of diamonds with the jack."

(XV)

NORTH
♠ A 6 4
♡ 8 2
◇ K Q 10 9 6 3
♣ 8 3

WEST
♠ J 9 3
♡ Q 9 4 3
◇ A 5 4
♣ K J 2

EAST
♠ 10 8 5 2
♡ J 7 5
◇ J 8
♣ Q 7 6 5

SOUTH
♠ K Q 7
♡ A K 10 6
◇ 7 2
♣ A 10 9 4

23. The Garozzo Tip

Benito Garozzo is the other half of the marvellous Garozzo–Forquet partnership. His Bols Tip related to the selection of your opening lead against a small slam contract and his advice coincides exactly with my feelings on the subject—attack!

"Heroic measures are rarely needed when leading against a game contract. The defenders can expect to get the lead again after the dummy has been exposed, and the early play will offer further clues to what they should do.

"Not so against slams. Unless two tricks can be cashed at once, the defence must strike a telling blow to develop the setting trick by the opening lead. Later is too late.

"The one factor that works in favour of the defence is that declarer is rarely willing to risk immediate defeat if any alternative seems attractive. And sometimes such an alternative can be created by the lead itself. For example, your right-hand opponent has bid to 6◇ on this auction:

NORTH	SOUTH
1♣	2◇
3♣	3◇
3♠	4NT
5♡	5NT
6♣	6◇
NB	

You hold:

♠ Q 9 5 2
♡ K 8 4
◇ J 5 3 2
♣ K J

"Obviously defensive prospects are poor. Not only is partner broke, but the cards are well placed for declarer. But do not despair. Take advantage of what you know that declarer doesn't know: trumps aren't breaking.

"Lead ♣J. The fact that you let him see ♣J makes it even more likely that he will be able to establish the suit with no more than a single loser. In fact, if you had three clubs you should deliberately choose the jack as your lead. The full hand:

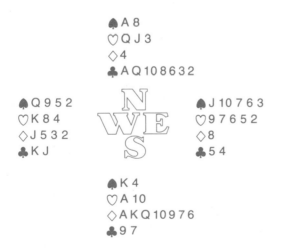

♠ A 8
♡ Q J 3
◇ 4
♣ A Q 10 8 6 3 2

♠ Q 9 5 2   ♠ J 10 7 6 3
♡ K 8 4   ♡ 9 7 6 5 2
◇ J 5 3 2   ◇ 8
♣ K J   ♣ 5 4

♠ K 4
♡ A 10
◇ A K Q 10 9 7 6
♣ 9 7

"Declarer knows he can establish the clubs by giving up a trick to ♣K, but why should he risk doing so immediately when there is a chance you may ruff? He goes up with ♣A and by the time he finds out he must lose a diamond trick it is too late. Any other lead forces him to make his contract.

"Not quite so clear is how to attack South's slam contract after the following bidding:

SOUTH	NORTH
1♢	1♠
2♣	3♢
3NT	4♣
4NT	5♡
6♢	NB

Your hand:

♠ K 7 6 2
♡ K 10 8 3
♢ 9 7 5
♣ 6 2

"It sounds as if the opponents may have reached a 'momentum' slam, which may not be reached at the other table. So it is even more important for you to defeat it with your lead. How much do you know?

"North is surely short in hearts and declarer has few spades, so a trump lead seems promising. But wait. Neither opponent has indicated long trumps and both seem long in clubs. With such deals it is rarely necessary to stop a crossruff, because declarer will be unable to cash enough tricks in his long side suit—in this case, clubs. However, if he needs to pick up a twelfth trick, you know that a spade finesse is going to succeed. How can you point him away from that line of play?

"What is partner going to contribute to the defence? From the fact that South didn't bid 5NT, you consider the possibility that his side may be missing an ace—if so, it is probably ♡A. If not, you must hope for ♡Q, because—yes, you are going to lead ♡K.

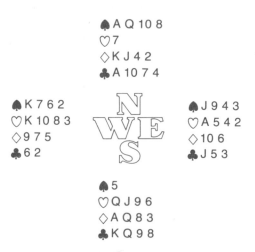

♠ A Q 10 8
♡ 7
♢ K J 4 2
♣ A 10 7 4

♠ K 7 6 2   ♠ J 9 4 3
♡ K 10 8 3   ♡ A 5 4 2
♢ 9 7 5   ♢ 10 6
♣ 6 2   ♣ J 5 3

♠ 5
♡ Q J 9 6
♢ A Q 8 3
♣ K Q 9 8

"When your ♡K holds the first trick, you switch to a spade. Declarer may decide that your lead has made it unnecessary for him to rely on the spade finesse. He can count twelve tricks if he can establish a heart trick via a ruffing finesse against your 'marked' ♡A, because he can ruff two spades and throw a third spade on the established heart trick. But when he ruffs a spade and leads ♡Q, finessing you for the ace, partner produces that card to defeat the slam.

"Given another lead, South virtually MUST take the winning spade finesse.

"My final example of an attacking lead against a slam contract is more difficult because it requires that you look a long way ahead and visualise the probable layout.

"A strong auction takes the opponents to 6♠:

NORTH	SOUTH
1NT	2♣
2♡	3♠
4♢	5♣
5♡	6♠
NB	

Your lead is from:

♠ 8 5 3
♡ K J 9 8
♢ 8 2
♣ K J 8 5

"Clearly, you hold most if not all of the defensive assets. Very likely ♣K will score one trick, but ♡K is almost surely badly placed. And if, after a winning heart finesse, declarer is still a trick short, you are vulnerable to a heart-club squeeze.

"Can this threat be successfully countered? Maybe. Lead a heart now, and again when you come in with ♣K. Which heart? A low one may (it does) allow declarer too cheap a trick if he has ♡10. An honour is preferable, and ♡K is best. As you have brilliantly figured out, this is the layout:

♠ K 10 2
♡ A Q 7 5
♢ A K
♣ 10 7 3 2

♠ 8 5 3   ♠ 7 6
♡ K J 9 8   ♡ 6 4 3
♢ 8 2   ♢ 10 7 6 5 4 3
♣ K J 8 5   ♣ 9 6

♠ A Q J 9 4
♡ 10 2
♢ Q J 9
♣ A Q 4

"Declarer is helpless after the lead of either heart honour. By continuing with the other honour when you gain the lead in clubs, you destroy dummy's heart entry and South can no longer squeeze you. As a result, in good time you will come to the two club tricks and the congratulations of the other players at the table.

"So, my Bols Tip is this: Games may be quietly defended, but slams must be *attacked*."

Having read Benito Garozzo's Bols Tip with great interest, I was amused to hear of the following hand from the *Harper's* and *Queen's*—Philip Morris Christmas Bridge Festival in December 1977.

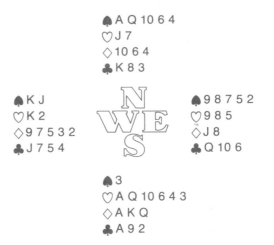

```
                    ♠ A Q 10 6 4
                    ♡ J 7
                    ◇ 10 6 4
                    ♣ K 8 3

      ♠ K J              N          ♠ 9 8 7 5 2
      ♡ K 2          W   E          ♡ 9 8 5
      ◇ 9 7 5 3 2        S          ◇ J 8
      ♣ J 7 5 4                     ♣ Q 10 6

                    ♠ 3
                    ♡ A Q 10 6 4 3
                    ◇ A K Q
                    ♣ A 9 2
```

When Warwick Pitch held the West hand, he heard the opponents bid as follows:

SOUTH	NORTH
2♡	2♠
2NT	3♡
4♣	6♡
NB	

Remembering Garozzo's advice, Warwick selected ♠J as his opening lead—with· devastating results. Declarer understandably decided to bank everything on the heart finesse, and he went up with ♠A and ran ♡J, eventually losing one heart and one club trick to go one down. On a more passive lead, of course, South would enter dummy with ♣K and finesse the heart. When this lost, he would fall back on the spade finesse to get rid of his losing club.

World champions in Rotterdam, Georgio Belladonna facing Bentio Garozza and playing against Hans Krevns and Bob Stavenburgh from the Netherlands.

And so to the final Bols Bridge Tip, No. 24. This was by Israel's Schmuel Lev, and, in my view, it was one of the best Tips in the entire series.

"One of the maxims which bridge took over from whist in its early days was 'Third hand plays high'. Another slogan that expressed exactly the same idea was 'Never finesse against your partner.'

"Since then, of course, a great deal has been discovered. My Bols Tip refers to some quite frequent situations where it can be very good play for third hand to 'finesse' against his partner—that is, to play the lower of non-touching honours even though dummy has a worthless holding in the suit led.

"A common situation occurs in no trumps (Fig. XVI). It is often vital to winkle out declarer's stopper on the first round, so that the suit can be cashed when defenders regain the lead.

"West leads ♣4 against South's contract of 3NT. If East puts up the ace ('Third hand plays high!'), South will duck the next round of clubs and West's suit will be dead. South will be able to develop his ninth trick by taking a heart finesse into the safe hand.

"But if East plays ♣J on the first round, it will appear to South that West may have the ace-queen and he will not know that it is safe to duck. South may therefore win the king and take the heart finesse. Now East continues clubs and beats the contract.

"Of course, there is sometimes an element of risk when you finesse against your partner. Here, East may give declarer an unnecessary trick if he holds ♣Q-x-x. But East can afford to take this risk, for he has control of the major suits and can see that the contract will be defeated if West's club suit can be brought in. East also knows that West cannot possibly have a side entry, and that the play of ♣J is therefore vital.

"Against a suit contract, a 'finesse' may create an entry for a vital switch.

(XVI)

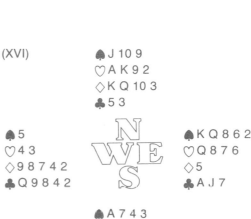

```
                    ♠ J 10 9
                    ♡ A K 9 2
                    ♢ K Q 10 3
                    ♣ 5 3
    ♠ 5                              ♠ K Q 8 6 2
    ♡ 4 3                            ♡ Q 8 7 6
    ♢ 9 8 7 4 2                      ♢ 5
    ♣ Q 9 8 4 2                      ♣ A J 7
                    ♠ A 7 4 3
                    ♡ J 10 5
                    ♢ A J 6
                    ♣ K 10 6
```

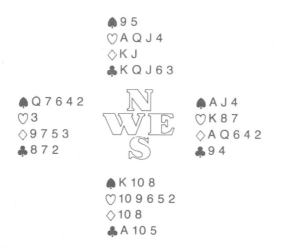

```
                    ♠ 9 5
                    ♡ A Q J 4
                    ♢ K J
                    ♣ K Q J 6 3
    ♠ Q 7 6 4 2                      ♠ A J 4
    ♡ 3                              ♡ K 8 7
    ♢ 9 7 5 3                        ♢ A Q 6 4 2
    ♣ 8 7 2                          ♣ 9 4
                    ♠ K 10 8
                    ♡ 10 9 6 5 2
                    ♢ 10 8
                    ♣ A 10 5
```

"South reaches 4♡ after North has opened with a Precision 1♣ and South has subsequently shown three controls—in this case, an ace and a king. West leads ♠4. If East makes the normal play of the ace, the contract will be made, declarer losing a spade, a heart and a diamond.

"East can see that a diamond from partner is vital, and he should therefore play ♠J at the first trick, driving out South's known ♠K. When East comes in with ♡K, he leads a small spade to his partner's queen. The obvious diamond switch now defeats the contract.

"A defender who has bid a suit may often have the opportunity to finesse against partner when this suit is led:

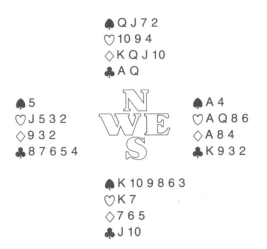

```
            ♠ Q J 7 2
            ♡ 10 9 4
            ◇ K Q J 10
            ♣ A Q

♠ 5                          ♠ A 4
♡ J 5 3 2         N          ♡ A Q 8 6
◇ 9 3 2        W     E       ◇ A 8 4
♣ 8 7 6 5 4       S          ♣ K 9 3 2

            ♠ K 10 9 8 6 3
            ♡ K 7
            ◇ 7 6 5
            ♣ J 10
```

"East opens with 1♡ but South becomes the declarer in 4♠. West leads ♡2, which suggests that he has an honour in the suit. East therefore finesses the queen, forcing the king. When East comes in with ♠A, it is quite safe to underlead ♡A, as West is expected to have the jack. Now West can find the vital club switch before ◇A is dislodged.

"If East makes the routine play of ♡A at the first trick, the defenders can never make more than their three aces.

"My Bols Tip is this: When you have a holding such as A-Q or A-J in the suit led by partner, do not automatically play 'Third hand high'. By finessing the lower honour, you may sometimes succeed in creating a vital entry to your partner's hand."

The Bols Tips Competitions have now come to an end. It is to be hoped that the twenty-four tips have been interesting and instructive to many players: this was, after all, the main reason for creating them.

To summarise, I feel that Jeff Rubens' tip was the best of an extremely good selection. In fact, as a result of reading his advice, I have developed a new slogan which I employ whenever one of my lady partners produces an obscure piece of defence: "Please, Mrs. Rubens, help me!"

The American Scene

THE AMERICAN SCENE

For a number of reasons, the USA took the lead in world bridge during and immediately after the Second World War. They seemed extremely difficult to beat at that time, but there was a great deal of bridge talent in Britain and other European countries and, by adopting some of the clever tactics and ideas which had been developed in the USA, we soon learned how to face them without feeling inferior. The USA won the Bermuda Bowl World Championship in 1950, 1951, 1953 and 1954, but Great Britain broke their hold in 1955. France kept the title in Europe by defeating the USA in 1956, and there then followed a remarkable string of successes by the invincible Italian Blue Team, who won the Bermuda Bowl on ten consecutive occasions between 1957 and 1969.

The USA obviously has a vast pool of players from whom to choose their national team, and the European countries simply have to make up in quality for what they lack in quantity. The traditional bidding methods used in the USA are normally described by the nebulous term "Standard American", and they are very similar to the methods advocated by Charles Goren. However, Goren's system incorporates forcing jump raises by the responder, for example 1♡–3♡, and there is an increasing tendency these days for US experts to adopt the principle of limit raises, which is such an inherent part of the Acol system.

Sub-Standard American

There are two common features of the Standard American system with which I have very little sympathy: the weak two opening bid and the principle that an opening bid of 1♡ or 1♠ should guarantee a five-card suit.

In my view, the weak two opening bid has two obvious drawbacks. First, it means that strong one- and two-suited hands which would be opened with a forcing two-bid in Acol have to be opened with a mere one-bid, and this inevitably results in a number of perfectly reasonable games and even slams being missed; furthermore, it requires the opener to make awkward jumps on the second round if he opens with a modest one-bid on a powerhouse hand and is fortunate enough to hear a response by his partner or an overcall by one of the opponents. The second drawback to weak twos is that they are rarely reserved for suitable hands. While I can see some point in opening with a pre-emptive bid of 2♡ on a hand of this nature:

♠ 7 2
♡ A Q J 9 5 4
◇ J 10 4
♣ 6 3

I have found by experience that most operators do not have sufficient patience to wait for that kind of hand to come along; they usually cannot resist opening with a weak two bid on entirely unsuitable hands, for example:

♠ K 7 2
♡ Q 10 8 5 4 2
◇ Q J 4
♣ 6

This can only lead to trouble.

Five-card majors also have serious theoretical drawbacks, as follows:

(a) They compel the opener to open the bidding on virtually non-existent minor suits. This is not too serious if he is able to bid a three-card club suit, but there are terrible problems if the opener's distribution is 4-4-4-1 or 4-4-3-2; he will be forced to open the bidding with 1◇, and this in turn will make life difficult if the initial response is 2♣.

(b) The need to make an unnatural opening bid on a three-card minor suit can prove fatal if the opponents eventually play the hand and your partner is on lead. For example:

♠ A K 7 4
♡ Q J 6 2
◇ J 4 2
♣ Q 7

If you are playing five-card majors and this hand does not fall within your 1NT range, you will have to open with the revolting bid of 1◇. If your left-hand opponent eventually becomes the declarer, your partner might well make a disastrous opening lead from something like ◇K-x or ◇A-x-x.

(c) While the system will probably work reasonably well in an uncontested auction, to open with a weak minor suit makes the opening side extremely vulnerable to pre-emption. For example, a 4-4 or longer heart fit can easily be lost if the opener has to open 1♣ or 1◇ and the next player is able to intervene in spades.

(d) The need to open with non-existent minor suits on certain hands will cause the responder to mistrust *all* opening bids of 1♣ or 1◇. He may therefore feel reluctant to make a natural raise if the opponents overcall in a major suit.

(e) The extended use of minor-suit openings gives more freedom to the opposition. An opening bid of 1♡ or 1♠ has distinct pre-emptive value and may make it difficult for the opponents to enter the auction.

The other worrying aspect of current US bidding methods is their concentration on complicated gadgets. As I mentioned in an earlier chapter, to play too many conventions places a great strain on the memory and, in my view, must have an adverse effect on other departments of your game. I feel that this criticism can be levelled with some justification at certain players on the other side of the Atlantic.

This amusing deal from the US Trials in 1976 is a good illustration of what I mean by players finding their gadgets a liability. South dealt at love all.

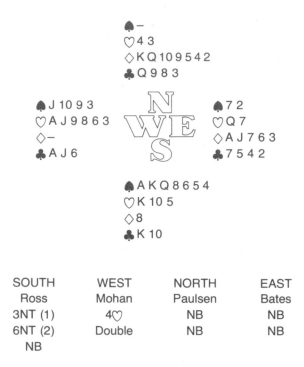

```
                    ♠ —
                    ♡ 4 3
                    ◇ K Q 10 9 5 4 2
                    ♣ Q 9 8 3
    ♠ J 10 9 3           N          ♠ 7 2
    ♡ A J 9 8 6 3     W     E       ♡ Q 7
    ◇ —                  S          ◇ A J 7 6 3
    ♣ A J 6                         ♣ 7 5 4 2
                    ♠ A K Q 8 6 5 4
                    ♡ K 10 5
                    ◇ 8
                    ♣ K 10
```

SOUTH	WEST	NORTH	EAST
Ross	Mohan	Paulsen	Bates
3NT (1)	4♡	NB	NB
6NT (2)	Double	NB	NB
NB			

(1) Showing a solid major suit.
(2) The unfortunate South thought that it was his partner who had bid 4♡, showing 5 controls.

The defenders slipped, and South escaped for the loss of −500. This still seemed unlikely to be a good result, but North-South actually gained 9 i.m.p. on the board. At the other table:

SOUTH	WEST	NORTH	EAST
Cohen	Hamilton	Katz	Eisenberg
3NT (1)	NB	4♡ (2)	NB
NB (3)	Double	NB	NB
NB (4)			

(1) Showing a solid major suit.
(2) Asking partner to pass or convert to 4♠, depending on his suit.
(3) Obviously under the impression that North had a long heart suit . . .
(4) . . . although he might have had second thoughts when 4♡ was doubled.

The defenders were not so kind against 4♡ doubled, and they extracted a penalty of 900.

Despite all my misgivings expressed above about five-card major openings and weak two bids, it is interesting to note that these methods became two principal features of the so-called Aces Scientific System—the system formulated by the famous Dallas Aces team, aided by a computer for research and experimentation. The Dallas Aces were a full-time professional bridge team, organised in 1968 by Dallas financier Ira Corn for the express purpose of bringing the World Team Championship back to the USA. In an attempt to duplicate the unity and team spirit of Italy's famous Blue Team, Corn selected six players from

America's leading young experts, paying each a salary, plus tournament expenses, to undertake a full-time career in studying and playing bridge. The first pair to be chosen were James Jacoby and Robert Wolff, and three other players, William Eisenberg, Robert Goldman and William Lawrence, accepted the offer in 1968; Robert Hamman, the sixth member, joined the team in 1969. Using a computer to analyse results and to generate specific sets of hands to provide practice in given areas of the game (slam hands, pre-emptive openings, etc.), the Aces spent 50–60 hours a week perfecting the three partnerships' bidding systems and discussing problems encountered at the table. Besides competing in national tournaments and regional team contests, the Aces played several practice and exhibition matches. In 1969, they won the Spingold Knock-Out Teams Championship and then routed the Vanderbilt champions by 141 i.m.p. in a play-off match to earn the right to represent the USA in the 1970 Bermuda Bowl in Stockholm. The Aces won the World Championship in 1970, returning the Bermuda Bowl to the USA for the first time since 1954, and successfully defended their world title in 1971; they were also runners-up in the World Championship in 1972, 1973, 1974 and 1975, although the composition of the team changed fairly frequently from 1971 onwards.

Here are two Aces, Goldman and Lawrence, in action in the Bermuda Bowl Final against Italy in 1973. North dealt with East West vulnerable.

```
                    ♠ A J 8 6 2
                    ♡ Q 10 7 6
                    ◇ Q J
                    ♣ K 5
  ♠ 10 9 4            N            ♠ K Q 7 3
  ♡ J 9          W       E         ♡ K 5
  ◇ A 9 6 4          S             ◇ K 10 2
  ♣ A 10 6 2                       ♣ J 9 7 3
                    ♠ 5
                    ♡ A 8 4 3 2
                    ◇ 8 7 5 3
                    ♣ Q 8 4
```

NORTH	EAST	SOUTH	WEST
Forquet	Goldman	Bianchi	Lawrence
1♠	NB	1NT	NB
NB (1)	NB		

(1) A dubious decision, in my view. Most British experts would rebid 2♡ on the North hand, and that would lead to a rather more comfortable contract.

West led ♣2, and dummy's ♣K held the first trick. South now played ♡A and another heart, and Robert Goldman was in with ♡K. The natural return at this point would be a second club, but Goldman realised that this might squander a trick if the defenders had four diamond tricks to cash. He therefore switched to ◇2. West won with ◇A and returned a second diamond, and this enabled East to cash ◇10 before pushing a club through. This thoughtful defence overcame the potential blockage in the diamond suit, and the unfortunate Bianchi was two down.

Robert Hamman brought in a bushel of points for the USA by making a tricky 4♡ contract on this deal from the 1974 Bermuda Bowl. In fact, he made six more tricks than his counterpart in the other room!

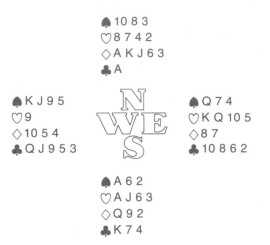

♠ 10 8 3
♡ 8 7 4 2
♢ A K J 6 3
♣ A

♠ K J 9 5　　♠ Q 7 4
♡ 9　　　　　♡ K Q 10 5
♢ 10 5 4　　　♢ 8 7
♣ Q J 9 5 3　　♣ 10 8 6 2

♠ A 6 2
♡ A J 6 3
♢ Q 9 2
♣ K 7 4

West led ♣Q to dummy's ♣A. At the second table, Hamman crossed to ♡A to ruff his losing club in dummy. He then played a small heart from dummy, and East won with ♡Q, West discarding a club. East returned a club to declarer's ♣K, and Hamman crossed to dummy with a diamond to play another heart. East went up with ♡K and returned another club, but South discarded a losing spade to remain in control of the situation. He won the spade switch with ♠A, drew the outstanding trump and cashed three more diamond tricks to land his contract.

As you will see, West misdefended by discarding a club on the second round of trumps. If he had retained his fifth club, he could have continued the forcing game for an extra round, and South would have been compelled to concede another trick.

Six down — 1 in smoke

At the other table, Boulenger was in the same 4♡ contract for France, and West, Robert Goldman, led ♠5. Declarer won with ♠A, crossed to ♣A and led a trump to ♡A. He then cashed ♣K, discarding a spade from dummy, and exited with a small trump, hoping for a 3-2 break. East, Mark Blumenthal who had joined the Aces in 1973, was now able to draw trumps and cash a number of black-suit tricks. When the smoke cleared, South had gone six down to concede −600.

A number of Aces and former Aces were involved when this hand (Fig. I) occurred in the Spingold Teams Championship in 1974. West dealt with North-South vulnerable.

(Fig. I)

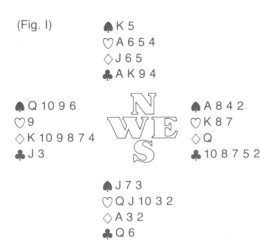

♠ K 5
♡ A 6 5 4
♢ J 6 5
♣ A K 9 4

♠ Q 10 9 6　　♠ A 8 4 2
♡ 9　　　　　♡ K 8 7
♢ K 10 9 8 7 4　♢ Q
♣ J 3　　　　♣ 10 8 7 5 2

♠ J 7 3
♡ Q J 10 3 2
♢ A 3 2
♣ Q 6

WEST	NORTH	EAST	SOUTH
Kantar	Swanson	Eisenberg	Soloway
NB	1♣	NB	1♡
2♢	3♡	NB	4♢
NB	4♡	NB	NB
NB			

Paul Soloway had replaced William Eisenberg in the Aces Team in 1971; Edwin Kantar and John Swanson joined the team in 1974.

West led ♠10, and South ducked in dummy. East won with ♠A and switched to ◇Q. Declarer won with ◇A and, faced with the prospect of losing ♡K, a diamond and a diamond ruff, he decided to play three top clubs first, in order to discard one of his losing diamonds. Unlucky. West ruffed the third club and cashed ◇K, and East later made ♡K for one down.

At the other table, West gave the show away by making a weak jump overcall.

WEST	NORTH	EAST	SOUTH
Jacoby	Reinhold	Lazard	Cohen
NB	1♣	NB	1♡
3◇	3♡	NB	4♡
NB	NB		

West led ♠10, and East won ♠A and switched to ◇Q as before. On this occasion, however, declarer knew for certain that ◇Q was a singleton, and he therefore played ♡A and another heart before touching the clubs. +620 to North-South.

Mrs. Edith Kemp, of Miami Beach, Florida, is one of the greatest American women players of all time. I first met her thirty years ago, and we have been friends ever since. I am a great admirer of her game, which resembles that of the very best male players. For example, consider this deal from the Philip Morris Cup Heat in Monte Carlo in 1977. North dealt at game all.

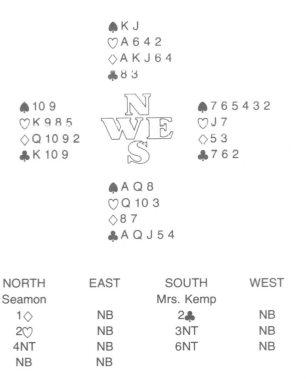

```
                    ♠ K J
                    ♡ A 6 4 2
                    ◇ A K J 6 4
                    ♣ 8 3
    ♠ 10 9                        ♠ 7 6 5 4 3 2
    ♡ K 9 8 5                     ♡ J 7
    ◇ Q 10 9 2                    ◇ 5 3
    ♣ K 10 9                      ♣ 7 6 2
                    ♠ A Q 8
                    ♡ Q 10 3
                    ◇ 8 7
                    ♣ A Q J 5 4
```

NORTH	EAST	SOUTH	WEST
Seamon		Mrs. Kemp	
1◇	NB	2♣	NB
2♡	NB	3NT	NB
4NT	NB	6NT	NB
NB	NB		

West led ♠10, and Edith won in dummy and finessed ♣Q, losing to West's ♣K. West returned a second spade, and declarer won in hand and successfully finessed dummy's ◇J. She then made the key play of cashing ♡A before playing off four rounds of clubs. This left the following position (Fig. II).

♠A now squeezed West in the red suits, and Edith Kemp was home.

(II)

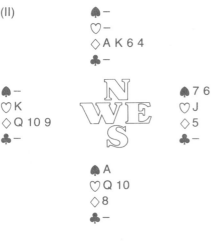

```
                    ♠ —
                    ♡ —
                    ◇ A K 6 4
                    ♣ —
    ♠ —                          ♠ 7 6
    ♡ K                          ♡ J
    ◇ Q 10 9                     ◇ 5
    ♣ —                          ♣ —
                    ♠ A
                    ♡ Q 10
                    ◇ 8
                    ♣ —
```

THE AMERICAN SCENE

One of the leading American male players in recent years has been Barry Crane, the television producer. Crane is considered by many to be the best match-pointed pairs player of all time, and he is the world's top master-point holder. This hand from the Pasadena Paris Championship of 1977 will give you some idea of why this is so. North dealt with North-South vulnerable.

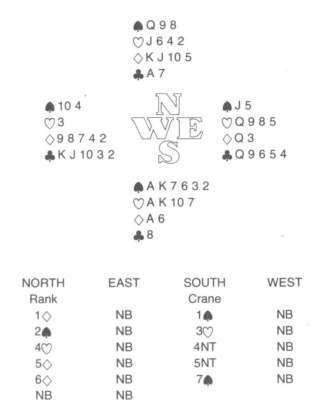

NORTH	EAST	SOUTH	WEST
Rank		Crane	
1♦	NB	1♠	NB
2♠	NB	3♡	NB
4♡	NB	4NT	NB
5♦	NB	5NT	NB
6♦	NB	7♠	NB
NB	NB		

West led ◇9, and declarer played ◇10 from dummy and captured East's ◇Q with ◇A. He drew trumps in two rounds, cashed dummy's two diamond winners and crossed back to hand with ♡A. ♡K and three more rounds of spades left the following end position:

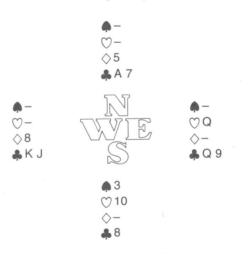

♠3 now effected a perfect double squeeze. West had to retain ◇8, East had to retain ♡Q, and neither of them could keep two clubs. Dummy's ♣A-7 therefore made the last two tricks.

Crane showed excellent technique on this hand. He could, of course, have finessed ♡10 to make his contract, but he was able to play two top hearts in an attempt to drop ♡Q from West first—knowing that if East held the guarded ♡Q, the double squeeze was bound to succeed.

One of North America's rising stars is Peter Nagy, who is of Hungarian origin but now lives in Montreal. An extremely poor bidding sequence gave him a chance to show his skill on the following hand from the Spingold Teams Championship in 1975. North dealt at game all.

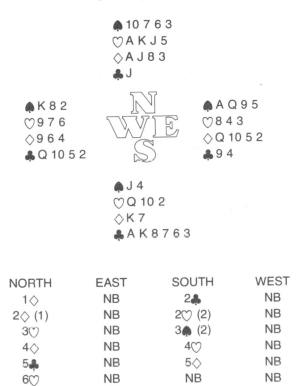

```
              ♠ 10 7 6 3
              ♡ A K J 5
              ◇ A J 8 3
              ♣ J

  ♠ K 8 2              ♠ A Q 9 5
  ♡ 9 7 6      N       ♡ 8 4 3
  ◇ 9 6 4    W   E     ◇ Q 10 5 2
  ♣ Q 10 5 2    S      ♣ 9 4

              ♠ J 4
              ♡ Q 10 2
              ◇ K 7
              ♣ A K 8 7 6 3
```

NORTH	EAST	SOUTH	WEST
1◇	NB	2♣	NB
2◇ (1)	NB	2♡ (2)	NB
3♡	NB	3♠ (2)	NB
4◇	NB	4♡	NB
5♣	NB	5◇	NB
6♡	NB	NB	NB

(1) This is a good illustration of the problems which arise when one plays five-card majors.
(2) South's major suit bids were probes for 3NT, but North clearly misunderstood.

Not surprisingly, West failed to find an opening spade lead. He led a trump, and Nagy won in dummy with ♡A, played a club to ♣A and ruffed a club high in dummy. A diamond to ◇K and another high club ruff were followed by a small heart to ♡10. ♡Q drew both outstanding trumps, and South cashed ♣K and another club, leaving the following end position (Fig. III).

South now cashed ♣7, throwing a spade from dummy. In order to avoid being thrown in to lead into dummy's diamond tenace, East discarded ♠A. However, declarer cashed ◇A and led ♠10 from dummy, and West was forced to win and give South his twelfth trick with ♠J.

This was a neat play by Peter Nagy, but the defence was not perfect. East should have discarded ♠A earlier and retained ♠Q, for he could then discard ◇5 when South led ♣7 in the diagram position shown right.

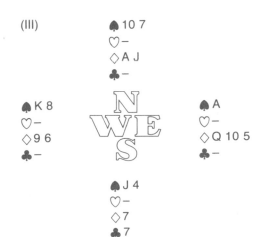

```
(III)          ♠ 10 7
               ♡ –
               ◇ A J
               ♣ –

  ♠ K 8                 ♠ A
  ♡ –          N        ♡ –
  ◇ 9 6      W   E      ◇ Q 10 5
  ♣ –           S       ♣ –

               ♠ J 4
               ♡ –
               ◇ 7
               ♣ 7
```

I described earlier how the Dallas Aces became the world's first full-time professional bridge team in 1968. They were followed by the Precision Team, a highly successful team of young experts from the New York City area who were sponsored by Charles Wei to play his Precision Club system between 1970 and 1973. The nucleus of this team was Steven Altman, Thomas Smith, Joel Stuart and Peter Weichsel, and they subsequently added David Strasberg, Eugene Neiger and Alan Sontag. The Precision Team had a number of major successes in US competitions, and four members of the team were invited to compete in the prestigious *Sunday Times* Pairs Championship in January 1973: Altman-Sontag and Smith-Weichsel finished first and second in the select 22-pair field, marking the first time a US pair had ever finished higher than fourth.

Here are Sontag and Weichsel in action in the 1977 Reisinger Memorial Trophy (Fig. IV). South dealt with East-West vulnerable.

(IV)

♠ K 3
♡ 10
◇ K J 10 5
♣ J 10 8 7 5 3

♠ Q J 4   ♠ A 10 9 6
♡ A K J 8 4   ♡ 9 3 2
◇ A 4 3   ◇ Q 8 7
♣ A K   ♣ 9 4 2

♠ 8 7 5 2
♡ Q 7 6 5
◇ 9 6 2
♣ Q 6

SOUTH	WEST	NORTH	EAST
	Sontag		Weichsel
NB	1♣ (1)	1♡ (2)	NB
2◇	2♡	NB	3♡
NB	4♡	5◇	Double
NB	NB	NB	

(1) A Precision 1♣ opening, showing 16+ points.
(2) Showing a major or minor two-suiter.

Sontag led ♡A and switched to a small diamond, won by his partner's ◇Q. Weichsel returned ♡9, and declarer ruffed in dummy and led a club to ♣Q and ♣K. West now played ◇A and another diamond, and that was the last trick that declarer made. Sontag-Weichsel were able to cash four spades, two hearts and one club to make eleven tricks in 5◇ doubled—a penalty of 2100.

The Precision Club system was devised by Charles Wei, a New York shipowner who was born in Shanghai. The system was used successfully by the Chinese team in the 1967, 1968 and 1969 Far Eastern Championships, and it attracted international attention when China reached the World Championship Finals in 1969 and 1970.

Precision ground

The principal features of the standard Precision system are as follows:

(a) An opening bid of 1♣ shows 16+ points. Suit responses, other than the negative 1◇, are positive, showing 8+ points and a five-card or longer suit. Balanced hands containing 8+ points are shown by responding in no trumps.

(b) An opening bid of 1NT shows 13–15 points.

(c) An opening bid of 1♡ or 1♠ shows 11–15 points and a five-card or longer suit.

(d) An opening bid of 1◇ shows 11–15 points and at least four diamonds.

(e) An opening bid of 2♣ is natural, showing at least five clubs and an unbalanced hand containing 11–15 points.

(f) An opening bid of 2◇ shows a three-suited hand with short diamonds.

(g) An opening bid of 2♡ or 2♠ is a weak two bid.

(h) A direct raise of a positive response to 1♣ is an asking bid, enquiring about the length and strength of the responder's trump suit; subsequent suit bids by the opener are also asking bids.

In its original form, the Precision Club system was fairly simple to learn and quite suitable for beginners at the game. By 1972, however, all three pairs of the famous Italian Blue Team were using their own versions of the system, and Belladonna and Garozzo have developed an incredibly complex variation entitled Super Precision. One example of Super Precision in action should be sufficient to show you what I mean:

WEST	EAST
♠ K J x	♠ A x x
♡ Q x x x	♡ K J 10 9 x
◇ A x x	◇ K J x
♣ A K Q	♣ x x

According to Belladonna and Garozzo, these hands should be bid as follows:

WEST	EAST
1♣ (1)	1♡ (2)
2♡ (3)	2NT (4)
3♡ (5)	3♠ (6)
4♣ (7)	4♠ (8)
4NT (9)	5◇ (10)
6♡ (11)	NB

(1) 16+ points with any distribution.
(2) 8+ points with at least five hearts.
(3) A trump asking bid in hearts.
(4) A step response showing five hearts to one top honour.
(5) A re-asking bid in hearts.
(6) A step response showing A-J, K-J or Q-J.
(7) A control asking bid.
(8) A step response showing four controls (ace = 2, king = 1).
(9) A cue bid in spades (!)
(10) A cue bid in diamonds.
(11) The final contract.

This sort of sequence makes me very grateful that I still play natural Acol methods.

It is impossible to discuss the Precision Club system without mentioning the fairy-tale story of Kathy Wei, Charles Wei's charming Peking-born wife. Her story has been told many times and there are many different versions, but here is mine. Charles married Kathy in 1968, when she was leading a very full and active life as the administrator of the medical facility of J. F. Kennedy Airport in New York. She had children from her previous marriage and, although Charles gave her the world, she found her life was becoming slightly empty as the children grew older and became more independent. She needed something to fill the gap, and Charles got to work and devised a special gift for his lovely wife: the Precision Club system. He invited her to be joint captain of the Chinese team in the World Championships in Rio in 1969 and, when her team did better than anyone had dared hope by finishing second to Italy, Kathy was hooked on bridge and on the Precision Club.

At this early stage, I must confess that I did not take the new system very seriously; in fact, I thought it was little more than an attractive toy for Kathy to play with. However, I had not reckoned with Charles Wei's business efficiency. He does not like failure, and he engaged some of the world's leading players and rewarded them for playing Precision—and for winning playing Precision.

Kathy's World triumph

It was not long before Kathy took the stage. She visited this country playing with Garozzo, Belladonna, Avarelli and Forquet, and I accompanied them to Manchester, where they played with great success in a number of exhibition matches and pairs tournaments. However, Kathy's greatest triumph came in the 1978 World Pairs Olympiad in New Orleans, when she and Judi Radin won the World Women's Pairs Championship – so Charles Wei's shrewd investment has once again paid handsome dividends.

While I have not become a convert to the Precision Club system, I have to admit that the Weis have given the bridge world a valuable new theory of bidding. It is significant that, alongside the Wei-Radin triumph in the Women's Pairs, the winners of the World Open Pairs Championship, Brazilian stars Gabino Cintra and Marcelo Branco, were also playing a version of Precision. It is difficult to argue with success but, while I think that a strong 1♣ system is quite suitable for somebody who is just starting bridge, it still seems to me that the Precision Club system has one or two serious weaknesses at the highest level. For example:

(a) It makes average opening hands which contain a club suit difficult to bid. They have to be opened with an unnatural bid of 1NT, with a ubiquitous bid of 1◇ or with a jump bid of 2♣, which only serves as a pre-emptive bid against your own side.

(b) The policy of only opening on five-card major suits leads to the difficulties which I listed earlier in this chapter, and these difficulties are magnified by the fact that there is no opening bid of 1♣ available. Far too great a burden is therefore placed on opening bids of 1◇ and 1NT.

(c) While the sequences which commence with a strength-showing bid of 1♣ work reasonably efficiently in an uncontested auction, Precision players are particularly vulnerable to pre-emptive tactics by their opponents. The days have passed when opponents used to sit politely back and admire the intricacies of the strong 1♣ systems. They now realise that they can intervene on slender values with very little danger of being doubled for penalties, and most players are now armed with conventional methods of disrupting the auction after a 1♣ opening.

(d) 16 points seems to me too low a minimum for a strong 1♣ bid. Bearing in mind that a positive response, which is made on as few as 8 points, is forcing to game, this means that a game-forcing situation might be created when there is no fit and a combined point count of only 24. This is one of the main reasons why, of all the strong 1♣ systems, I favour the Blue Club; the Blue Club requirement for a 1♣ bid is a good 17 points and, moreover, the development of the auction after a 1♣ bid proceeds in a fairly natural manner. Having said that, however, I am glad that most players have not introduced complicated systems and gadgets to the rubber bridge table. It would be a terrible bore if they were to do so. And, worse, most of the paying customers would simply disappear.

The Champions

THE CHAMPIONS

There are really two distinct games of bridge. There is rubber bridge, the game which is played in people's houses and in clubs which cater for money players. And there is duplicate bridge, which is the competitive or tournament game played by those who ignore the gambling aspect of bridge and prefer to match their skill and judgement against others who are struggling with the identical hands.

When capital counts . . .

In my view, rubber bridge and duplicate bridge are equally important, and a truly expert player should be able to master both divisions of the game. In practice, however, most players are markedly better at one game or the other, and this is the result of a number of different factors, particularly temperament. Like any other businessman, a rubber bridge player cannot prosper without the necessary capital, and he must have sufficient funds behind him to enable him to suffer a loss or two at his chosen stakes. A tournament bridge player, on the other hand, does not usually need a great deal of money.

Tournament bridge in the USA has grown to such an extent that they regularly hold congresses with as many as 16,000 tables in play. These congresses are usually held in hotels which are specially built for conventions and the like and which offer reasonable amenities at reasonable prices. There are no monetary rewards for the winners in these US events, and master points seem to be the most valuable currency in circulation. In fact, as I mentioned in Chapter 2, many experts offer their services for hard cash as partners for lesser players who wish to collect master points and achieve certain ranks. This practice is now rapidly spreading to other countries, including Great Britain.

Most other countries, except Britain, offer substantial cash prizes for winning important events, and there are usually other valuable prizes for those who finish near the top. I used to be rather disturbed about the effect which large money rewards would have on the game, but I can see now that they have contributed substantially to the enormous growth of competitive bridge all over the world.

. . . and character counts

I am often asked to name the best players in the world today, but I find it more and more difficult to give a sensible answer: there are so many good players in so many different countries. Furthermore, the standard of the average players is improving steadily all the time. I like to think that this is partly because they read instructive material written by people like me, but it is also because they learn by playing against good opposition. There is no greater pleasure for a relatively unknown pair than to win a tournament in which master players are competing, and this is quite likely to occur in a short-distance event. The longer the competition lasts, however, the more likely it is that the well-known players will prevail.

I shall be giving a list of some of the world's best players later in this chapter, but I must emphasise that I can only rely on my own knowledge and experience and that there are a few champions whom I have never had the pleasure of meeting. Furthermore, I might be biased towards a certain type of player, for good bridge technique alone is not enough for me: I also give credit for style, ethics and behaviour towards partners, team-mates and opponents. In this connection, I always found that the great Italian Blue Team were perfect gentlemen at the table, and I was surprised to find that their latin temperaments permitted them to show

Paul Chemla – partnering Omar Sharif – one of his favourite partners as well as mine.

commendable calm and coolness during the game. I have rarely seen them flare up during actual play, and it was only during the post-mortems at the end of the session that the discussions ever became at all heated.

Another reason why I might be slightly biased in my choice of top players is that I have a number of favourite partners. I love playing with good players who remain calm and have a favourable influence on my own performance by persuading me to remain calm as well. Raymond Brock is one partner of mine who never bats an eyelid and who brings out the best of my bridge, and this is indicated by our excellent results together. Benito Garozzo used to by my favourite partner until he began to expect and demand perfection.

My world of bridge

When I am playing rubber bridge, I hold the view that to finish on the winning side is an indication of a good performance. When the day comes and I cease to win at bridge, I hope I shall realise that my ability is waning and that the time has come to stop. This is probably one of the reasons why I have turned to writing about the game, and although I still thoroughly enjoy a good game of bridge and a pleasant partnership with a champion player, I also like to report international bridge events and record interesting hands. I love travelling the world in pursuit of bridge, and it is great fun to meet all those great players, a lot of whom I am proud to number among my good friends. Once they are away from the table, most of the top players are charming people. Some of them are under considerable strain while they are playing, but they all relax after the game and there is a great deal of enjoyment to be derived on these occasions.

One of the best advertisements in favour of bridge as a principal hobby is that a bridge player hardly ever needs to feel lonely; wherever he goes to play, he can guarantee finding company and friends, and bridge is a common bond with a language of its own.

THE CHAMPIONS

And now for my list of the world's top players, so that you will know who is being discussed when you read their names in bridge publications. Sweden is one of the richest bridge countries, for they have an abundance of young talent and they are the current European champions. The names to watch out for in Swedish bridge are Brunzell, Lind, Goethe, Morath, Sundelin and Flodqvist.

Sven-Olov Flodqvist earned 10 i.m.p. for Sweden on the following hand from the 1974 European Championships in Israel. South dealt at love all.

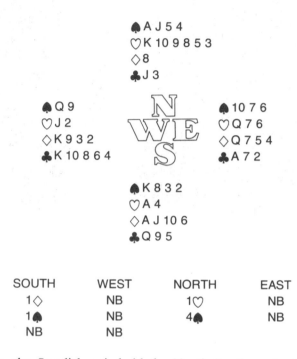

♠A J 5 4			
♡K 10 9 8 5 3			
◇8			
♣J 3			

SOUTH	WEST	NORTH	EAST
1◇	NB	1♡	NB
1♠	NB	4♠	NB
NB	NB		

When the Swedish pair held the North-South cards, the declarer made the obvious eleven tricks in 4♠. When Flodqvist and his partner were defending at the other table, however, they started with three rounds of clubs. South won the third round with ♣Q and cashed ♠K, on which Flodqvist dropped ♠Q from the West hand.

Convinced that the adverse trumps were divided 4–1, South decided to set about establishing dummy's hearts. He carelessly failed to draw a second round of trumps first, and continued with ♡A, ♡K and a heart ruff. To declarer's horror, West over-ruffed this trick with ♠9 and played a fourth round of clubs, promoting East's ♠10 as the setting trick.

Poland, who won the Rosenblum Teams Trophy at the New Orleans Olympiad in 1978, are led by Lebioda, Wilkosz, Macieszcak, Klukowski and Polec.

Poland's Janusz Polec played the following hand with excellent technique and just the right amount of cunning. North dealt at love all.

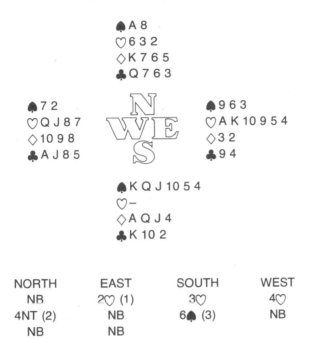

```
              ♠ A 8
              ♡ 6 3 2
              ◇ K 7 6 5
              ♣ Q 7 6 3

  ♠ 7 2              N        ♠ 9 6 3
  ♡ Q J 8 7       W   E      ♡ A K 10 9 5 4
  ◇ 10 9 8          S        ◇ 3 2
  ♣ A J 8 5                  ♣ 9 4

              ♠ K Q J 10 5 4
              ♡ -
              ◇ A Q J 4
              ♣ K 10 2
```

NORTH	EAST	SOUTH	WEST
NB	2♡ (1)	3♡	4♡
4NT (2)	NB	6♠ (3)	NB
NB	NB		

(1) A Weak Two Bid.
(2) The Unusual No Trump, asking South to choose between the two minor suits. 6◇ would have proved to be an easy contract . . .
(3) . . . but the lure of South's spade suit was too great.

West led ♡Q and Polec ruffed. At first sight, 6♠ seemed to depend on finding ♣J in the East hand. Since East was known to have at least six hearts, however, he was not very likely to hold a specific card in clubs, and Polec decided to try for an endplay instead. If West could be stripped down to ♣A-J-x and no other cards, South could succeed by leading ♣K from hand. There was just one snag. West probably held four hearts, which could not all be ruffed away, and he would therefore have to be persuaded to throw one of them away before the endplay could succeed.

If South had crossed to ♠A and ruffed a heart, West would probably have scented an endplay and would not have parted with a long heart. Polec therefore played off three rounds of trumps first, just as if an elimination had not even crossed his mind. On the third trump, West naturally discarded his fourth heart – and he was doomed. South cashed ◇A-Q, overtook ◇J with ◇K and ruffed a heart. ◇4 to ◇7 and another heart ruff set the scene for the endplay, and ♣K from hand now left West in a hopeless position.

The current French stars are Lebel, Chemla, Tintner, Roudinesco, Stoppa, Svarc, Farahat and Boulenger.

Jean-Michel Boulenger found a simple but excellent play on the following hand, dealt by North with North-South vulnerable.

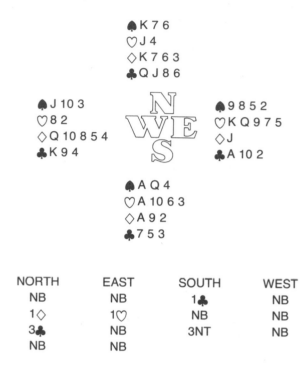

♠ K 7 6
♥ J 4
♦ K 7 6 3
♣ Q J 8 6

♠ J 10 3
♥ 8 2
♦ Q 10 8 5 4
♣ K 9 4

♠ 9 8 5 2
♥ K Q 9 7 5
♦ J
♣ A 10 2

♠ A Q 4
♥ A 10 6 3
♦ A 9 2
♣ 7 5 3

NORTH	EAST	SOUTH	WEST
NB	NB	1♣	NB
1♦	1♥	NB	NB
3♣	NB	3NT	NB
NB	NB		

West leads ♥8, and the declarer's natural reaction is to play ♥4 from dummy, thereby ensuring two heart tricks for himself. If he does so, East will insert ♥9 and South will win with ♥10. He needs two club tricks for his contract, but when he leads a small club towards dummy, West will go up with ♣K and return his second heart. This enables East to drive out ♥A while he still has ♣A as an entry, and the contract will fail.

It is true that declarer can duck East's ♥9 at the first trick, but he cannot then ensure the two heart tricks which he needs for his contract. Boulenger solved the problem when the hand occurred in actual play. He made the unnatural play of ♥J from dummy at trick one and allowed East's ♥Q to win. He won East's heart return with ♥10, and West now had no heart left to return when he gained the lead with ♣K; East's heart suit was therefore immobilised and Boulenger had given support to one of my pet theories about the game – that some of the best plays are also the simplest.

The leading lights in Austria are Rohan, Kirner, Strafner, In der Maur, Meinl and Manhardt.

Peter Manhardt was at his brilliant best on the following hand (Fig. I).

He became the declarer in the ambitious contract of 6♥, and West led ♠J. Manhardt finessed dummy's ♠Q and unblocked with ♠9 when ♠Q lost to East's ♠K. East switched to a trump, which ran to dummy's ♥8. Declarer concluded from East's failure to switch to a diamond that he was likely to hold ♦K, and his first move was to run ♦Q from dummy. This was covered with ♦K and ♦A, and South now finessed dummy's ♠8 and discarded his losing diamond on ♠A. ♦9 from dummy followed, and declarer ruffed away East's ♦J and drew trumps with dummy's ♥A-K.

(Fig. I)

♠ A Q 8
♥ A K 8
♦ Q 9 8 2
♣ A 5 4

♠ J 10 5
♥ 7 6
♦ 7 6 5 3
♣ Q 10 7 3

♠ K 7 6 4 2
♥ J 4 2
♦ K J 4
♣ 9 6

♠ 9 3
♥ Q 10 9 5 3
♦ A 10
♣ K J 8 2

This was the position after dummy's ◇8 was cashed:

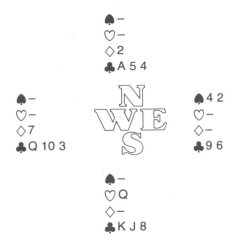

```
                    ♠ –
                    ♡ –
                    ◇ 2
                    ♣ A 5 4
      ♠ –                        ♠ 4 2
      ♡ –          N             ♡ –
      ◇ 7       W     E          ◇ –
      ♣ Q 10 3     S             ♣ 9 6
                    ♠ –
                    ♡ Q
                    ◇ –
                    ♣ K J 8
```

From the fall of the cards so far, Manhardt had good reason to believe that West's distribution was 3-2-4-4. He therefore elected to play for the squeeze: a club to ♣K followed by ♡Q left West completely without resource.

Among the excellent players in the Netherlands are Kreyns, Van Besouw, Kokkes and Slavenburg, and Switzerland can boast Catzeflis, Besse, Bernasconi and Patino.

I could fill another book by listing all the top-class players in the USA, but my particular favourites are Kantar, Eisenberg, Wolff, Hamman, Rubin, Kaplan and Kay, plus Murray and Kehela from Canada.

This hand from the 1978 World Pairs Olympiad in New Orleans shows Sammy Kehela and Eric Murray in effective action (Fig. 11). West dealt at love all.

WEST	NORTH	EAST	SOUTH
	Kehela		Murray
NB	1♣	1♡	1♠
4♡	NB	NB	4♠ (1)
NB	NB	NB	

(II)

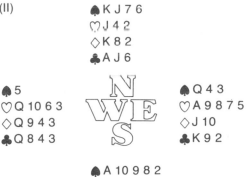

```
                    ♠ K J 7 6
                    ♡ J 4 2
                    ◇ K 8 2
                    ♣ A J 6
      ♠ 5                        ♠ Q 4 3
      ♡ Q 10 6 3     N           ♡ A 9 8 7 5
      ◇ Q 9 4 3   W     E        ◇ J 10
      ♣ Q 8 4 3     S            ♣ K 9 2
                    ♠ A 10 9 8 2
                    ♡ K
                    ◇ A 7 6 5
                    ♣ 10 7 5
```

(1) A typical Eric Murray bid. West's imaginative leap to 4♡ put the Canadian pair under pressure, but Murray thought that his side could make game somewhere – so he bid it.

When declarer first saw dummy, he realised that his prospects of bringing home ten tricks were remote: he seemed likely to lose one heart, one diamond and two clubs, and there was also ♠Q to be found. West led ♡3, and East won with ♡A and switched to ◇J, taken by dummy's ◇K. After a moment's deliberation, Murray cashed ♠K, dropping ♠8 under it, and ran ♠6 from dummy. When this held the trick, he cashed ♠A and ducked a diamond, compelling East to win with ◇10.

The situation for which Murray was hoping actually existed. If East led a club, declarer would lose only one club trick. East therefore returned a heart, and South discarded a club, allowing West to win with ♡Q. That set up dummy's ♡J for the discard of South's remaining club, and Murray was home. Instead of losing two clubs, one diamond and one heart, declarer had lost two hearts and one diamond – but no clubs.

Britain's leading players are currently Priday, Rodrigue, Flint, Sheehan, Rose, Hoffman, Brock, Rimington and Rosenberg, and we seem to be in the fortunate position of having a number of young players who are beginning to make a name for themselves.

Italy's top stars have won so many titles that their names have become like household words to anyone who follows the game of bridge: Forquet, Avarelli, Pabis-Ticci, Vivaldi, Franco, d'Alelio, and, of course, the legendary Garozzo and Belladonna.

Bridge publications of recent years have never been short of brilliant plays by Benito Garozzo to report. Here is one one my favourite Garozzo hands, dealt by East at game all.

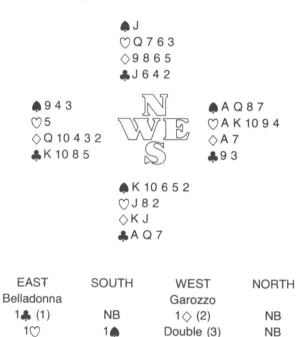

♠ J
♡ Q 7 6 3
◇ 9 8 6 5
♣ J 6 4 2

♠ 9 4 3　　　　　♠ A Q 8 7
♡ 5　　　　　　　♡ A K 10 9 4
◇ Q 10 4 3 2　　◇ A 7
♣ K 10 8 5　　　♣ 9 3

♠ K 10 6 5 2
♡ J 8 2
◇ K J
♣ A Q 7

EAST	SOUTH	WEST	NORTH
Belladonna		Garozzo	
1♣ (1)	NB	1◇ (2)	NB
1♡	1♠	Double (3)	NB
NB	NB		

(1) Precision, showing 16+ points and any distribution.
(2) Negative, showing 0–7 points.
(3) A Sputnik double, suggesting the two unbid suits.

West led ♡5 against 1♠ doubled, and East won with ♡K and switched to ♣9. Declarer ducked and West won with ♣K and returned a second club. South now played a small spade to ♠J, and East won, cashed ♡A and gave his partner a heart ruff. A third round of clubs enabled East to ruff, leaving the position shown in Fig. III.

East now played ♡10, and declarer ruffed with ♠10. If Garozzo had made the natural play of discarding a diamond at this point, South would have exited with a trump and endplayed West, forcing him to lead a diamond or a club. However, Garozzo was alive to the dangers: he under-ruffed with ♠9! When South now played a trump, East was able to win with ♠8, cash ♠A and exit with the last heart, forcing declarer to ruff and open up the diamond suit himself. This brilliant defence made the penalty + 1,100.

(III)　　　♠ –
　　　　　♡ Q
　　　　　◇ 9 8 6 5
　　　　　♣ J

♠ 9　　　　　　　♠ A 8
♡ –　　　　　　　♡ 10 9
◇ Q 10 4 3　　　◇ A 7
♣ 10　　　　　　♣ –

♠ K 10 6 5
♡ –
◇ K J
♣ –

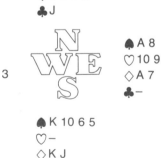

And here is superstar Giorgio Belladonna in action in the 1959 World Championship.

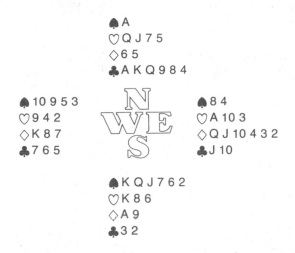

```
                    ♠ A
                    ♡ Q J 7 5
                    ◇ 6 5
                    ♣ A K Q 9 8 4
    ♠ 10 9 5 3        N           ♠ 8 4
    ♡ 9 4 2      W         E       ♡ A 10 3
    ◇ K 8 7          S           ◇ Q J 10 4 3 2
    ♣ 7 6 5                       ♣ J 10
                    ♠ K Q J 7 6 2
                    ♡ K 8 6
                    ◇ A 9
                    ♣ 3 2
```

At one table in the Italy v USA match the American North-South pair played in 4♠ and made an overtrick.

At the other table, a weak 2◇ opening by East caught Belladonna and Avarelli off balance, and they reached the unlikely contract of 6♡, played by the South hand. West led ◇7 and when declarer's ◇A was removed at the first trick, any hope he had of making 6♡ seemed to have vanished.

However, Belladonna made it look easy. He won ◇A, crossed to ♠A and played three top clubs. The third club was ruffed by East with ♡10, and declarer over-ruffed with ♡K. He then cashed ♠K, discarding dummy's diamond loser, and ran ♡6 from his hand. When this drew ♡A from East and the hearts were revealed to have been 3-3 originally, declarer was home and Italy had achieved another slam swing.

The best and most famous Tournament Director of them all – Harold Franklin.

THE CHAMPIONS

Who does not know Omar Sharif? The occasion was Sunday Times *event – January 1979*

Three top international players hail from Egypt: Gresh, Yallouze and, of course, the one and only Omar Sharif, the famous film star who has the happy knack of playing well with almost any partner.

Omar Sharif first judged well in the bidding of the following freak hand, and then followed it up by some shrewd cardplay. South dealt with East-West vulnerable.

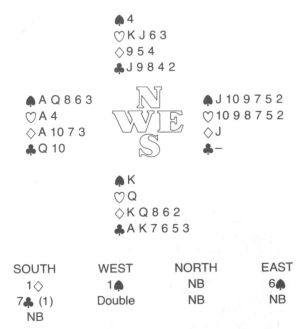

```
                    ♠ 4
                    ♡ K J 6 3
                    ◇ 9 5 4
                    ♣ J 9 8 4 2

♠ A Q 8 6 3          N            ♠ J 10 9 7 5 2
♡ A 4           W         E       ♡ 10 9 8 7 5 2
◇ A 10 7 3           S            ◇ J
♣ Q 10                            ♣ –

                    ♠ K
                    ♡ Q
                    ◇ K Q 8 6 2
                    ♣ A K 7 6 5 3
```

SOUTH	WEST	NORTH	EAST
1◇	1♠	NB	6♠
7♣ (1)	Double	NB	NB
NB			

(1) East's violent leap to 6♠ made the remainder of the auction a complete guess. However, Sharif acted on the assumption that his vulnerable opponents must know what they were doing, and he was right – West would have made twelve tricks with little difficulty.

At first sight, it looks as if declarer must lost four tricks in 7♣ doubled – one spade, one heart and two diamonds. However, careful play cut the loss to a mere 500 points. West cashed his two major suit aces and continued with a second round of hearts. Sharif won with ♡K in dummy, drew trumps in two rounds and crossed to dummy with ♣J to play a diamond to ◇K. West correctly ducked to avoid being endplayed, and Sharif now crossed to dummy with a trump to cash ♡J, leaving the following position:

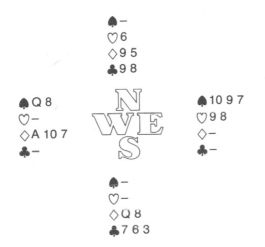

```
              ♠ –
              ♡ 6
              ◇ 9 5
              ♣ 9 8
  ♠ Q 8         N        ♠ 10 9 7
  ♡ –         W   E      ♡ 9 8
  ◇ A 10 7      S        ◇ –
  ♣ –                    ♣ –
              ♠ –
              ♡ –
              ◇ Q 8
              ♣ 7 6 3
```

Sharif had a complete count on the clubs and hearts, and the bidding and play strongly suggested that East's original distribution was 6-6-1-0 rather than 5-6-2-0. He therefore led a heart from dummy, discarding a diamond from the closed hand, and East was endplayed; he was forced to concede a ruff and discard in hearts or spades, and Sharif was able to throw his remaining diamond loser while he ruffed in dummy.

Germany's leading players are all well-established: von Dewitz, Chodziesner, Rummel, Auhagen, Schroeder, Prinz Waldeck, Gynz and Piekenbrock. However, Germany also has a great many outstanding young players who are showing considerable promise.

Previous Dutch and English teams flank Rixi Markus at her annual Guardian Easter *tournament.*

The world's top three countries in women's bridge today are probably Britain, the USA and Italy. The players whom I respect most in this country are Fritzi Gordon, Jane Priday, Sandra Landy and Nicola Gardener, but there are a number of comparative newcomers who I am certain will make it to the very top.

Nicola Gardener, who is often described as the youngest veteran in bridge, found a very thoughtful defence on this deal:

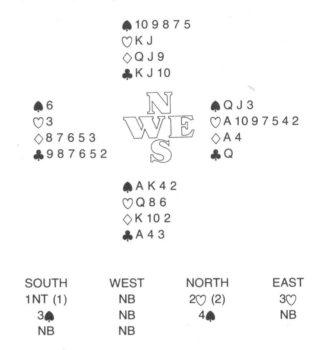

	♠ 10 9 8 7 5	
	♡ K J	
	♢ Q J 9	
	♣ K J 10	

SOUTH	WEST	NORTH	EAST
1NT (1)	NB	2♡ (2)	3♡
3♠	NB	4♠	NB
NB	NB		

(1) 15–17 points.
(2) A transfer bid, requesting the opener to convert to 2♠. North planned to rebid 3NT over 2♠, thereby showing a balanced hand containing five spades.

West led ♡3 to ♡J and ♡A, and Nicola paused to consider which heart she should return for her partner to ruff: whichever card she played would obviously be interpreted as a suit preference signal. Since she could not possibly want a club return, ♡2 would be highly suspect. However, if West put her in with ♢A, she would obviously be expected to lead another heart; and since West obviously could not ruff higher than dummy, the trump position would be given away and declarer would take two spade finesses.

Nicola solved the problem by cashing ♢A before giving her partner a heart ruff. With no entry to hand left to betray her, she was able to sit back and await a trump trick to defeat the contract.

From the USA, I would select Carol Sanders, Kerri Shuman, Mary Jane Farell, Dorothy Truscott, Judi Radin, and Kathy Wei, and from Italy Anna Valenti and Marisa Bianchi.

I regret to say that I cannot mention every bridge-playing country and its champion players without overflowing into another book. However, I would just like to mention in conclusion that Hungary at last seems to be coming back as a power in world bridge, and that Denmark and Norway can always be relied upon in European events.

I have never been in Mexico but I am aware that they can field a strong team led by their champion Dr. George Rosenkranz, equally well known as an inventor of a system and author of bridge books.

The Old Masters

THE OLD MASTERS

There was a great upsurge in competitive bridge at the end of the Second World War. As far as Europe was concerned, Great Britain reigned supreme, and we won the European Open Championship three years in succession—1948–1950.

There were two principal reasons for this British supremacy. The first, and possibly the more important, was that Great Britain had become the home of many talented card players who had fled from the Bolsheviks and the Nazis. These players either became members of the Great Britain team or succeeded in raising the standard of our home-grown players by their ability or by their contributions to bidding theory.

This last point provides a clue to the second reason for British supremacy—our bidding systems were dynamic and, having undergone considerable development, had many advantages over pre-war Culbertson. Keen minds had been instrumental in designing the Acol, CAB and Baron systems, all of which were based on natural approach-forcing principles. Even today, over 30 years later, Acol is still the most popular bidding system in Britain. To quote the late S. J. Simon, one of its principal architects, the Acol system is really an "attitude of mind"; in other words, it has a loose structure with certain rigid features. Acol remains a primarily natural system, based on the variable no trump, strong two bids and limit raises. It is, however, continually being enhanced by the incorporation of new concepts from other more modern systems. No discussion of Acol would be complete without mentioning the late Ian MacLeod, who was one of the great players responsible for the development of the system.

I would now like to discuss some of the exploits of the stalwarts of the golden era of British bridge. A hand from the 1948 Great Britain–Ireland European championship match springs to mind; South dealt with North-South vulnerable.

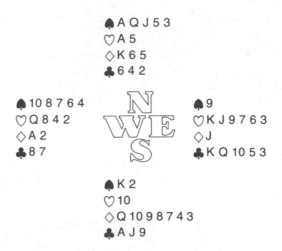

Boris Schapiro and Terence Reese, arguably the best pair who have ever played for Great Britain and probably the best pair in the world in 1948, were sitting in the North-South seats. The bidding sequence was:

SOUTH	WEST	NORTH	EAST
(Schapiro)		(Reese)	
1◇ (1)	NB	1♠	2♡
NB	3♡	3NT	4♡
5◇	NB	NB	5♡ (2)
Double (3)	NB	NB	NB

(1) Schapiro's bid of 1◇ is a typical Acol light opening.
(2) The Irish pair did well to push on to 5♡, for 5◇ would almost certainly be made; in fact, only an opening club lead defeats 6◇.
(3) This double was well judged. The British pair collected the obvious +100.

In the other room, the Irish bidding tactics were questionable.

SOUTH	WEST	NORTH	EAST
	(Rayne)		(Konstam)
3◇	NB	5◇	5♡
6◇	Double	NB	NB
NB			

South's pre-emptive opening bid with good defensive strength is not to my liking but it propelled the Irish pair into the excellent contract of 5◇. The late Kenneth Konstam, "Konnie" as he was affectionately known, was not one to sit on the fence and his interference bid of 5♡ was typical of the man.

When South took the strange action of bidding 6◇, it was the turn of young Eddie Rayne to rise to the occasion. 6♡ would be the normal action with his hand, but Rayne doubled and then found the killing lead of ♣8.

Declarer won the first trick and played on spades to try to get his club losers away. Konstam ruffed the second round and cashed ♣K. He then gave his partner a club ruff. With ◇A still to come, the British had savagely taken 800.

It was a great loss to British bridge when, for business reasons, Eddie Rayne's great talent was lost to the competitive game.

Here is Konstam in action again (Fig. I) – as a dummy player. This hand, dealt by West at love all, occurred in the Great Britain v. Norway match in the European Championships.

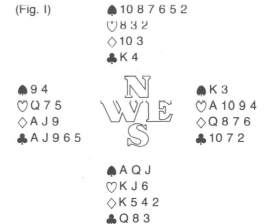

(Fig. I)

♠ 10 8 7 6 5 2
♡ 8 3 2
◇ 10 3
♣ K 4

♠ 9 4
♡ Q 7 5
◇ A J 9
♣ A J 9 6 5

♠ K 3
♡ A 10 9 4
◇ Q 8 7 6
♣ 10 7 2

♠ A Q J
♡ K J 6
◇ K 5 4 2
♣ Q 8 3

WEST	NORTH	EAST	SOUTH
	(Dodds)		(Konstam)
1♣	NB	1♡	NB
2♡	NB	NB	2♠ !
NB	NB	2NT	NB
NB	3♠	NB	NB
NB			

Konstam passed on the first round, no doubt hoping to double the possible no trump rebid, but he was thwarted by West's raise to 2♡. His bid of 2♠ would not have occurred to many players, but Konstam always followed hunches. Leslie Dodds, another great player destined to become a World champion with Konstam in 1955, showed great restraint in passing 2♠, but he persisted with 3♠ over East's 2NT.

♡5 was led to ♡A, and ◇6 was returned. Konstam played low, and West won with ◇J. A trump was then led and ♠A took East's ♠K. A low club to dummy's king followed, and then another trump. ♣Q put West on play. After a slight trance he exited with ♣J, but declarer discarded dummy's diamond. West now had to give a trick and the contract.

THE OLD MASTERS

In the same event, there was an interesting Acol sequence in Great Britain's match against Denmark. South dealt at game all.

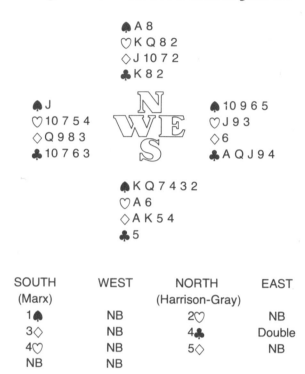

	♠ A 8	
	♡ K Q 8 2	
	◇ J 10 7 2	
	♣ K 8 2	

♠ J		♠ 10 9 6 5
♡ 10 7 5 4		♡ J 9 3
◇ Q 9 8 3		◇ 6
♣ 10 7 6 3		♣ A Q J 9 4

	♠ K Q 7 4 3 2	
	♡ A 6	
	◇ A K 5 4	
	♣ 5	

SOUTH	WEST	NORTH	EAST
(Marx)		(Harrison-Gray)	
1♠	NB	2♡	NB
3◇	NB	4♣	Double
4♡	NB	5◇	NB
NB	NB		

Two more of Britain's famous players were involved at this table. Maurice Harrison-Gray, captain of the Great Britain team, decided to bid 2♡ in preference to the "book" bid of 2◇ or 3NT. When Jack Marx bid 3◇, which was completely forcing, Gray could not adequately describe his hand. He therefore borrowed the "fourth-suit forcing" concept from the Baron system and tried 4♣. Marx gave preference to 4♡, but Gray then showed his true colours with 5◇, and Marx correctly passed.

The declarer play was also first class. A club was led to ♣9 and a trump returned to ◇Q. A second club forced declarer to ruff, and ◇A disclosed the bad split. Marx abandoned trumps for the moment, and crossed to dummy with a spade to ruff dummy's last club with ◇K. ♡A and another heart permitted declarer to draw trumps and claim his contract. This very neat example of reverse dummy play, the concept of which I introduced to you in Chapter 5, brought in a bushel of match-points when the Danes reached the bad contract of 6♠ and were deservedly defeated.

Terence Reese has always been an original thinker at the game and he was the first player to demonstrate that there are certain situations in which one can make a psychic bid and profitably stand the double. This hand from the Open Trials in 1951 was dealt by West with North-South vulnerable (Fig. II).

Reese's team-mates, Alan Truscott and Robert d'Unienville, bid the North-South cards accurately to Seven Hearts, and scored 2,210 without difficulty. At Reese's table the bidding went:

(II)

	♠ A K Q 10	
	♡ K 6 4 2	
	◇ J 9 5 3	
	♣ J	

♠ J 9 8 7 5		♠ 6 3
♡ 9 3		♡ 10 7
◇ 10 8 6 2		◇ Q 4
♣ 8 2		♣ K 10 9 7 6 4 3

	♠ 4 2	
	♡ A Q J 8 5	
	◇ A K 7	
	♣ A Q 5	

WEST	NORTH	EAST	SOUTH
(Schapiro)	(Dodds)	(Reese)	(Pavlides)
NB	1♠	1NT	Double
NB	NB	NB	

As Reese explained later, he interposed a whimsical 1NT "psike". When this was doubled, he decided to pass instead of running to 2♣. "I played with great tenacity, but I was unable to record a trick. Seven down, 1,300 to the opponents," wrote Reese in the Contract Bridge Journal. Jordanis Pavlides, the great Greek player who emigrated to Britain, was South on this hand. It is easy with hindsight to criticise his double and state that 2NT is a better solution, but this was the conclusion of the pundits of the day. Pavlides' great day was yet to come—he was a member of Great Britain's World Championship team in 1955.

Great Britain again won the European Championship at Montreux, Switzerland, in 1954, and this gave us the right to play USA for the World Championship in New York in 1955. In the 1954 match between Great Britain and Italy, there was a deal on which the late Adam Meredith, another world champion to be, made two calamitous mistakes concurrently at trick one; South dealt at love all.

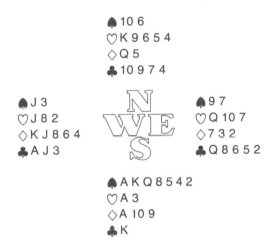

```
                    ♠ 10 6
                    ♡ K 9 6 5 4
                    ◇ Q 5
                    ♣ 10 9 7 4

    ♠ J 3                          ♠ 9 7
    ♡ J 8 2          N             ♡ Q 10 7
    ◇ K J 8 6 4    W   E           ◇ 7 3 2
    ♣ A J 3          S             ♣ Q 8 6 5 2

                    ♠ A K Q 8 5 4 2
                    ♡ A 3
                    ◇ A 10 9
                    ♣ K
```

The Italians in the North-South seats reached the terrible contract of 6♠ after a series of artificial bids. Meredith, sitting West, was obviously bored by the tedious bidding machinery and he found the only lead to give the contract—the jack of trumps. This allowed declarer to win, set up the heart suit with one ruff and re-enter dummy with ♠10. In my view, the odds against the British player finding such a bad lead were at least 25 to 1 against. If these odds look strange, you must bear in mind that Meredith made two mistakes when he led ♠J, for it was not his lead! South had opened with an artificial bid of 1◇ to show a big hand and North had responded 1♠ to show one control—the king of hearts.

THE OLD MASTERS

The following hand from the 1955 World Championship clash between the United States and Great Britain indicates both the difference between Acol and the American style of bidding and also the efficiency of Reese and Schapiro in defence. North dealt at game all.

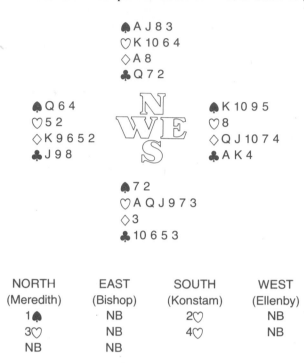

♠ A J 8 3
♡ K 10 6 4
◇ A 8
♣ Q 7 2

♠ Q 6 4
♡ 5 2
◇ K 9 6 5 2
♣ J 9 8

♠ K 10 9 5
♡ 8
◇ Q J 10 7 4
♣ A K 4

♠ 7 2
♡ A Q J 9 7 3
◇ 3
♣ 10 6 5 3

NORTH	EAST	SOUTH	WEST
(Meredith)	(Bishop)	(Konstam)	(Ellenby)
1♠	NB	2♡	NB
3♡	NB	4♡	NB
NB	NB		

♣9 was led to ♣K, and East switched to ◇Q, West signalling with ◇5. Konstam drew trumps and then led a low spade from the table. East played the king, cashed ♣A and led another diamond, but there was no diamond trick to be had: 620 to Great Britain.

In the replay the British got into the bidding:

NORTH	EAST	SOUTH	WEST
(Rosen)	(Schapiro)	(Mathe)	(Reese)
1♣	1◇	1♡	2◇
2♡	2♠	4♡	NB
NB	NB		

The prepared 1♣ bid both allowed Schapiro to enter the bidding cheaply and warned the defenders off leading the suit. Furthermore, if the British had been so inclined they could have sacrificed in 5◇ for one down. As it was, they were happy to defend. Reese opened with ♠Q, and declarer played ♠A and cashed one round of trumps. ◇A and a diamond ruff came next. A trump to dummy was followed by a low spade. Schapiro won with ♠9 and had a problem which he solved by leading ♠K. Mathe ruffed, but ♠J was of no use to him. He led a trump to dummy and discarded a club on ♠J. A low club was then led, but Schapiro ducked and Reese won the trick. Two further club tricks were readily available for one down.

Here is another hand from the 1955 World Championship match between Great Britain and the USA, which Great Britain won by 5,420 points. West dealt with North-South vulnerable.

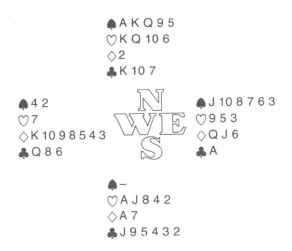

```
            ♠ A K Q 9 5
            ♡ K Q 10 6
            ◇ 2
            ♣ K 10 7

  ♠ 4 2            N         ♠ J 10 8 7 6 3
  ♡ 7         W         E    ♡ 9 5 3
  ◇ K 10 9 8 5 4 3     S     ◇ Q J 6
  ♣ Q 8 6                    ♣ A

            ♠ –
            ♡ A J 8 4 2
            ◇ A 7
            ♣ J 9 5 4 3 2
```

The British bidding, with the opponents silent, was as follows:

NORTH	SOUTH
(Konstam)	(Meredith)
1♠	2♡
4♡	6♡
NB	

Adam (Plum) Meredith was one of the fastest players of bad contracts I have ever seen; when the contract was good, however, he often took his time, and he did just that on this occasion. ◇ 10 lead was won in hand and two top trumps cashed. Three top spades were then played, declarer discarding clubs. When West showed out on the third round, East was known to have nine cards in the major suits; Meredith therefore drew the outstanding trump and made the percentage play of finessing the ♣ J for +1,430.

There would seem to be little opportunity for a swing on this board, but this is what happened in the other room:

WEST	NORTH	EAST	SOUTH
(Schapiro)	(Ellenby)	(Reese)	(Roth)
3◇	Double	4◇	6♣
NB	NB	NB	

Schapiro led his singleton heart and the contract was doomed. This was yet another example of aggressive Acol bidding making life difficult for the opponents.

THE OLD MASTERS

Albert Rose and Nico Gardener were two more of our great players of the immediate post-war era. They initially belonged to the Baron school of bidding and, although they each played with many other partners, they were probably at their most effective when playing together. Here is a good defensive hand from the 1958 Gold Cup Final. South dealt at game all.

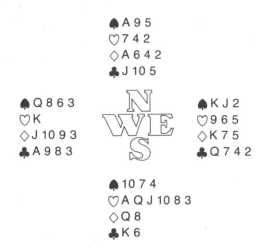

♠ A 9 5
♡ 7 4 2
◇ A 6 4 2
♣ J 10 5

♠ Q 8 6 3
♡ K
◇ J 10 9 3
♣ A 9 8 3

♠ K J 2
♡ 9 6 5
◇ K 7 5
♣ Q 7 4 2

♠ 10 7 4
♡ A Q J 10 8 3
◇ Q 8
♣ K 6

Rose led ◇J against South's contract of 2♡. Dummy played low and Gardener won with ◇K. Nico realised that dummy's spade entry must be attacked immediately, and he therefore returned ♠K in case declarer held the queen. ♠A won and a losing trump finesse was taken. Rose cashed ♠Q and led another to East's ♠J. Many players at this stage would return a club, in which case the fate of the declarer's contract will depend on the view he takes. Nico thought more deeply than that, and he returned a diamond. Declarer now had two views to take. First he had to guess whether the trumps were 3-1 or 2-2. If they were 3-1, he must overtake ◇Q with ◇A and then try to guess the club position. If they were 2-2, South could win ◇Q, draw the outstanding trumps and cross to dummy with ♡7 to discard a club on ◇A. In practice, declarer misread the position and Nico's "odds-on" shot had paid off.

My golden group

There were many outstanding bridge players in this country during that Golden Era. I expect I shall foolishly omit one or two obvious names, but I would like to pay special tribute, in alphabetical order, to the following: Leslie Dodds, Nico Gardener, Maurice Harrison-Gray, Kenneth Konstam, Jack Marx, Adam Meredith, Jordanis Pavlides, Terence Reese, Albert Rose, Boris Schapiro, Skid Simon, Joel Tarlo and Louis Tarlo. In those days, in fact, it became difficult to select a team because there were so many good players to choose from. Incidentally, I do not regard it as a coincidence that most of these players also played rubber bridge: I have always maintained that playing bridge for money is an excellent grounding for tournament players.

The State of the Game

THE STATE OF THE GAME

The basic organisation of bridge has been developed on similar lines to that of most physical sports like golf and tennis.

The tournament game in this country is largely organised by the English Bridge Union, which was founded in 1938 as the successor to the Duplicate Bridge Control Board. The E.B.U. runs a great many national events, the most important of which are the Life Masters Pairs, the National Pairs and the Crockfords Cup, and it has a current membership of over 20,000 players.

The E.B.U. is in turn a constituent member of the British Bridge League, which was founded in 1931 by A. E. Manning-Foster. The B.B.L. has been a federal body since 1938, and its other chief constituents are the Northern Ireland Bridge Union, the Scottish Bridge Union and the Welsh Bridge Union; India, New Zealand and South Africa are also affiliated to the League. The B.B.L. selects British teams for European Championships and world events, and it also organises the Camrose Trophy for home international competition, the prestigious Gold Cup for open teams, the Portland Cup for mixed pairs and the Lady Milne Cup for women's teams.

'Euro' bridge

The B.B.L. sends delegates to the European Bridge League, which was founded in 1947 by eight countries: Belgium, Denmark, Finland, France, Great Britain, Netherlands, Norway and Sweden; membership has since grown to a total of twenty-five countries. For thirty years or so after the end of the Second World War, the European Championships were held annually, apart from the four years in which there was a World Team Olympiad. Since 1977, however, the European Championships have become a biennial event. There was a pre-war European Federation which ran annual contests.

In 1958, the E.B.L. combined with the American Contract Bridge League and Australian Bridge Council to form the World Bridge Federation. One of the most prominent figures in European and World bridge, Baron Robert de Nexon, helped to realise this ambitious scheme. The W.B.F. aims to provide a central organisation to bind together all the national controlling bridge institutions of the world. It arranges a World Olympiad Teams Championship every four years, a World Olympiad Pairs Championship every four years, and the Bermuda Bowl World Teams Championship every odd-numbered year.

On top of the World

The most recent major event to be organised by the World Bridge Federation was their fifth quadrennial Pairs Olympiad, held in New Orleans in 1978. This event was enjoyed by many, and it was a pleasure to have two weeks of hard-fought bridge, smoothly run and unmarred by controversy. The first event, the prestigious Open Pairs, was held over ten sessions: two qualifying stages and a four-session final. The title was won by the Brazilian world champions, Marcelo Branco and Gabino Cintra.

At the same time as the Open Pairs, the seven-session Ladies Pairs was taking place, and this was won by the US pair, Kathy Wei and Judi Radin. Next came the Mixed Pairs event, which was won by the hot favourites from the USA, Barry Crane and Kerri Shuman. The Ladies' World Team Championship, the Venice Cup, also went according to the formbook, for the USA (Mary Jane Farell and Marilyn Johnson, Emma Jean Hawes and Dorothy Truscott, Jacqui Mitchell and Gail Moss) defeated the Italian ladies in the final.

The final event of the New Orleans fortnight was the new Rosenblum Cup, the world knock-out team championship. The complicated format worked out extremely well, producing two strong semi-final matches in which Poland defeated France and Brazil defeated the USA. Poland went on to rout Brazil in the final to take the championship.

This hand (Fig. I), from the Venice Cup Final, was played with her usual expert efficiency by Italy's Marisa Bianchi.

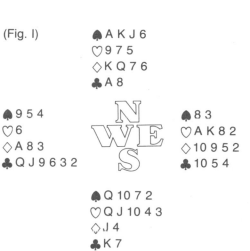

(Fig. I)
♠ A K J 6
♡ 9 7 5
♢ K Q 7 6
♣ A 8

♠ 9 5 4   ♠ 8 3
♡ 6   ♡ A K 8 2
♢ A 8 3   ♢ 10 9 5 2
♣ Q J 9 6 3 2   ♣ 10 5 4

♠ Q 10 7 2
♡ Q J 10 4 3
♢ J 4
♣ K 7

WEST	NORTH	EAST	SOUTH
3♣	Double	4♣	4♡
NB	NB	NB	

West led ♣Q and declarer won in dummy and played a small heart to ♡10, which held. A trump to dummy's ♡9 was taken by East, who drove out South's ♣K. If Marisa Bianchi had now made the lazy play of crossing to dummy with ♠A to lead another heart, she would have lost control; East would go up with ♡A and fire back a third club, reducing declarer to an equal number of trumps before she had established her diamond trick. However, South saw the danger. She led ♢J first, driving out West's ♢A, and the defenders were now powerless.

At the other table, there was no pre-empt by the Italian West player. The US pair bid efficiently to 4♠, the four-four fit—only to be defeated by the obvious heart ruff.

Two of my favourite hands from New Orleans came first and second in the Bols Brilliancy Competition for the most brilliant play or defence of the fortnight. First prize went to Gilles Cohen of Paris for a marvellous deception in the Open Pairs semi-finals (see Fig. II). East dealt at love all.

(II)
♠ A Q 8 6 2
♡ 3
♢ A J 9 7 5 2
♣ 6

♠ K J 10 7   ♠ 5 4 3
♡ A 8 5   ♡ J 10 7 2
♢ K 10 8   ♢ 4
♣ 9 8 5   ♣ K Q J 10 7

♠ 9
♡ K Q 9 6 4
♢ Q 6 3
♣ A 4 3 2

EAST	SOUTH	WEST	NORTH
Souchon	Mayer	Cohen	Frendo
NB	NB	NB	1♠
NB	2♡	NB	3♢
NB	3NT	NB	NB
NB			

Cohen led ♠J against 3NT, and Italian star Federico Mayer successfully finessed dummy's ♠Q. Declarer led a heart to ♡K, which lost to the ace, and Cohen battled on with ♠K. Mayer won and, to avoid cutting himself off from dummy, quite rightly tackled diamonds by leading low to ♢Q.

If West had won with ♢K, South would have made 3NT for a very good match-point score. However, Cohen ducked, playing ♢10 and apparently assigning ♢K to a useless death under the A-J. Declarer led a second diamond and Cohen followed with ♢8.

It seemed most unlikely to Mayer that West had ducked with ♢K. It seemed much more likely that East had ducked with ♢K-x, which would obviously be the correct play in certain circumstances. Mayer therefore rose with ♢A on the second round, expecting to drop East's ♢K and make a vital overtrick. When East showed out, the hand collapsed and Mayer was two down.

Perhaps Mayer should have played safe for nine tricks by finessing ♢J on the second round. However, the facts are that he did not, and that he would certainly have made the contract if Cohen had not been brilliant enough to duck with ♢K in this unusual position.

(III)

```
          ♠A 9
          ♡Q 9 8 4 2
          ◇J 10 6 3
          ♣K 8
♠K J 6 5     N        ♠10 7 4
♡A J 5    W     E     ♡10 7 6
◇9 5 2       S        ◇K 7 4
♣10 9 6               ♣Q J 5 4
          ♠Q 8 3 2
          ♡K 3
          ◇A Q 8
          ♣A 7 3 2
```

Second place in the 1978 Bols Brilliancy Competition went to Billy Eisenberg of Los Angeles, who was in the West seat when this deal occurred in the Teams event (Fig. III).

SOUTH	WEST	NORTH	EAST
1NT	NB	2◇ (1)	NB
2♠	NB	3♡	NB
3NT	NB	NB	NB

(1) Forcing Stayman.

As everybody knows, the general rule of defence is that the second player should normally play low. However, there are exceptional circumstances in which the correct defence is to play a high card, and on the above deal Eisenberg proved that it is even best on occasions to play Second Hand Middle.

Eisenberg led ♣10 against 3NT, and declarer won with ♣K in dummy, finessed ◇Q and led a low heart towards dummy—on which West played the jack! South won with ♡Q in dummy, ran ◇J and led a third diamond to ◇A. He then exited with ♡K, and Eisenberg won with ♡A. He continued with ♣9, which held the trick, and another club drove out South's ♣A.

A spade to ♠A enabled dummy to cash the last diamond, and a third heart was led from dummy. Because of West's earlier unblock, East was able to win this trick with ♡10. He cashed ♣Q and played a spade through, and declarer was two down. If Eisenberg had not unblocked on the first round of hearts, he would have been forced to win the third round with ♡J and concede the game-going trick to South's ♠Q. Similarly, if he had failed to unblock originally and subsequently attempted to recover by discarding ♡J on the fourth diamond, South would still prevail. He would simply lead ♠9 from dummy, covering if East covers, and he must once again come to that elusive ninth trick.

Finally, an opening lead problem from the Pairs Olympiad, correctly solved by the French star Jean-Marc Roudinesco. He had to lead after the following auction:

Dealer South; East-West vulnerable

SOUTH	WEST	NORTH	EAST
Roudinesco		Stoppa	
NB	NB	1♠	3NT
4♣	NB	NB	4NT
NB	NB	NB	

His hand was:

```
♠Q J 6
♡A
◇4 2
♣J 10 9 7 5 3 2
```

Roudinesco realised that East must have a long, solid diamond suit and guards in the black suits, and he therefore reasoned that there might be a weak spot in hearts. ♡A followed by a spade switch enabled his partner to cash one spade and two more hearts to defeat the contract by one trick. East would have made eleven tricks in comfort after an original spade lead, because the defenders would not be able to get at their three heart tricks.

One of the recent achievements of the World Bridge Federation has been to assist in revising the Laws of Duplicate Bridge. The Laws of Contract Bridge and of Duplicate Bridge had been revised by the Portland Club, the European Bridge League and the National Laws Commission of the American Contract Bridge League in 1963, but the 1975 revision of the Duplicate Laws under the auspices of the A.C.B.L. and the W.B.F. effectively made them into the first truly worldwide code. The new laws seem to me to be completely fair and sensible, and there is just one small alteration which I would like to see made: in my view, once a hand has been dealt, there should be complete silence at the table apart from the bidding and any related questions about bidding methods; to eliminate some of the extraneous comments would also avoid some of the unpleasant incidents which spoil everyone's enjoyment of the game.

Team topics

I mentioned a little earlier in this chapter that one of the principal functions of the British Bridge League is to select British teams for various international events. It almost goes without saying that these selections have caused a considerable amount of controversy over the years; moreover, some of this controversy has either directly or indirectly concerned me, and I feel very strongly about the methods of selection which should be employed. I am sure that I could fill several pages, if not several chapters, on this thorny subject, but this is neither the time nor the place for such a discussion. I would just like to make one or two constructive points which I am certain would do much to ease the difficulties and avoid a repetition of some of the unfortunate happenings of earlier years. These are my ideas:

(1) The tournament players themselves should have much more say in how bridge is run and how teams and their captains are selected.

(2) There should be a permanent trainer for both the Men's and Ladies' teams.

(3) The teams should be selected first and then consulted before captains are appointed.

(4) The traditional view is that the Ladies' Team should always have a male captain. However, we should perhaps consider appointing a female captain for the Ladies' Team, for she might prove to be more understanding towards the players. Furthermore, this might avoid some of the undercurrents, jealousies and love affairs which have sometimes occurred in the past.

(5) There should be no personal relationship between the members of a team and their captain.

(6) The team and captain should not be permitted to drink while "on duty" in an important championship.

Whenever I am discussing teams and captains, it is difficult for me not to think back to the bridge scene in Vienna between 1935 and 1937. At that time, we had a marvellous captain and team trainer in the famous lawyer Dr. Paul Stern. He was a very keen bridge player, and he simply could not be surpassed as a trainer. He insisted that both the Open and Ladies' teams should all play the same system, and this led to the obvious advantage that we were all completely interchangeable.

The stars of the Austrian team at that time were Dr. Edouard Frischauer, who was probably the most brilliant of them all and whose style can only be compared with that of Benito Garozzo among current players; Walter Herbert, who made a perfect partner for Frischauer; and Karl Schneider and Hans Jellinek, who were considered to be one of the greatest partnerships of all time. Jellinek fled to Norway at the outbreak of the Second World War but was captured by the Nazis when they invaded Norway and sent to the Auschwitz gas chambers. Other members of the Open Team were von Bluhdorn, Dr. von Kaltenegger, von Meissl, Fleischmann and Pollak.

Our Austrian Ladies' Team at that time was Marianne Boschan, Lise Klauber, Gretl Joseffy, Hella Mandl, Ethel Ernst, Gertie Brunner and myself. We won the European Championship in Brussels in 1935 and in Stockholm in 1936, and we took the World Championship in Budapest in 1937. We had been selected to represent Austria in Oslo in 1938, but Hitler's Anschluss shattered our dream of further triumphs and we were forced to remain the Team Which Was Never Defeated.

I have very happy memories of that pre-war Austrian team. We were known as "The Goats" and we wore our "Goat Brooches" with considerable pride. As well as playing well, we had an excellent team spirit and we were all great friends. If one member of the team suffered a setback of any kind, the rest of the team suffered with her and there was rarely any trace of jealousy. I was the youngest member of the team at that time, but the others all treated me with respect and accepted the fact that I was one of the important links in the team.

Standing is the late Howard Schenken one of the greatest players to ever come from the United States of America.

I arrived in London in March 1938, labelled as a refugee from Nazi oppression. Fortunately, my parents had come to London two years earlier, and I therefore had a ready-made home for my little girl and myself. I already had a number of contacts in British bridge circles, including Leslie Dodds, Kenneth Konstam, Graham Mathieson and Alfred Manning-Foster, the President of the British Bridge League. I was advised to join Almack's Club in Savile Row, where the standard of bridge was very high and where I was welcomed with open arms. I soon made many more friends, and my command of the English language improved steadily. I was also forunate in that Captain Edmond Pollak, who was British by birth but who had lived in Austria and had played in their famous Open Team, returned to England at that time, and he looked after me and taught me all there was to know about my strange new country.

My greatest partner

One of the nicest members of our bridge circle during the war was the shoe king Papa Rayne, as we called him. His young son Edward also joined us, and it soon became apparent that he was a potential star of the future. Edward's poor eyesight kept him out of the armed forces, and he was therefore able to become a member of our wartime team. The other players were Graham Mathieson, Leslie Dodds, Ewart Kempson and Walter Copley Carr. Walter was probably the best bridge partner I have ever had. He was one of the sons of Sir Emsley Carr, the Fleet Street newspaper king, and he died during the war after being invalided out of the Royal Air Force with an incurable blood disease.

Our wartime team scored a number of successes, but we were seriously lacking in young players and, while the USA was making great progress in the bridge world, we were not keeping up to date with all the new ideas and developments. My first visit to the States was at Christmas 1947, when I travelled a great deal and met all the great American bridge stars. Sam Stayman and I agreed that he would get together a strong US team to play against us and to give us the experience we so desperately needed. They finally came to this country in May 1949, and their team was Sam Stayman, the late Johnny Crawford, George Rapee and Peter Leventritt—a very powerful squad. We fielded the best team we could from the London area, including Leslie Dodds, Kenneth Konstam, Adam Meredith, Bob and Jim Sharples and myself, and to our great surprise and delight we beat the US team in a very friendly match. This result gave the British players a great boost in their confidence.

The bridge brain-drain

As I mentioned in Chapter 11, Great Britain had a number of great players in the immediate post-war years, and we achieved a number of memorable successes. Since the early 1960s, however, we have hardly won anything at all in men's competition, although we have had one or two near misses. The loss through ill-health of two of our brilliant newcomers, John Collings and Jonathan Cansino, has been a serious blow to our national team, and there has also been a miniature bridge brain drain to other countries, depriving us of the services of the late Adam Meredith, Ronald Crown, Alan Truscott and others.

Fortunately, Great Britain has done much better in women's bridge during the same period, and we have had sufficient talent in Fritzi Gordon, Jane Priday, Dorothy Shanahan, "Dimmie" Fleming, Joan Durran, "Penguin" Evans, Phylis Williams and others to beat the best teams from all over the world, including the USA. For example, we won the Ladies' Pairs and Mixed Teams at the 1962 Olympiad, and the Ladies' Team Olympiad in New York in 1964. I have also had a considerable amount of personal success during this period, and I consider myself extremely fortunate to have had some of the world's best players as my partners.

Looking now at the 1979 scene, we find that we have a great number of talented young players in this country, and it was very heartening to record a British victory in the Junior European Championships in Stirling in 1978. This event, along with many others, was sponsored by the National Bank of Dubai, whose General Manager, David Mack, M.B.E., can be described as a bridge-loving Scotsman. He spends several months in Europe each year, and we often play together in international competitions. Although David is not able to devote as much time to bridge as some others of us do, he is a very successful player. His friend and fellow-Scot Charles Bowman is a person who devotes a lot of time and money to bridge, and he organised the Junior European Championships in Stirling to the great satisfaction of everybody.

My view is that we can now look ahead to a brighter future for British bridge in open events. We also have great hopes in the women's field, for we have a very special talent in Nicola Gardener and there are several other girls who only need a little more experience and confidence before they begin to show the world that they can win bridge honours for Britain. It has always been my ambition to train a world-beating British ladies' team, but it seems that women tend to have more respect for a male coach and it is generally believed that there is less tension in the team when there is a man at the helm.

ACKNOWLEDGEMENTS

The publishers would like to thank the following organizations and individuals for their kind permission to reproduce the photographs in this book:

The *Guardian* 17; Rixi Markus 12, 31, 36, 39, 45, 51, 58, 61, 86, 98, 100, 103, 114, 139, 154; Malcolm Robertson 2, 6, 8, 10, 15, 21, 27, 43, 53, 67, 75, 85, 117, 129, 131, 137, 138, 141, 149.

Index compiled by Frederick Smyth

INDEX

Bold type indicates the more important references. *'bis'* means that there are two separate references on the one page; *'passim'* denotes that references appear throughout the pages numbered; 'q.' stands for 'quoted'.